"I am greatly honored that Ve[...] of this good book. It helps us t[...] [...] as a collection of individual truths, but as an organism in which each element of the gospel can be seen as a 'perspective' on others. The gospel is the same familiar message that it has always been, but in Vern's exposition it gives us even more amazement, astonishment, and fruitful applications for our living."

John M. Frame, Professor of Systematic Theology and Philosophy Emeritus, Reformed Theological Seminary

"If you enjoy watching a master craftsman at work on something he loves, telling you the things he finds fascinating about it, then you will love this book. Vern Poythress lovingly rolls the theme of truth over and over in his mind and then explains its beauty and depth with a simplicity that is accessible to everyone. This book is both mentally enriching and spiritually edifying, presenting core truths of Scripture from angles many of us have never considered. Read, reflect, and give God praise!"

Marcus A. Mininger, Professor of New Testament Studies, Mid-America Reformed Seminary; author, *Uncovering the Theme of Revelation in Romans 1:16–3:26*

"This volume is written with the clarity and insight we have come to appreciate from Vern Poythress. It provides an edifying examination of major biblical doctrines and their intrinsic harmony by considering them in terms of the theme of their truthfulness."

Richard B. Gaffin Jr., Professor Emeritus of Biblical and Systematic Theology, Westminster Theological Seminary; author, *In the Fullness of Time*

"'Truth is what God knows.' Beginning with this God-centered definition of truth, Vern Poythress explains how every major doctrine in systematic theology and every event in the world can be understood more deeply if we ponder its relationship to truth. Such a 'truth perspective' leads to numerous fresh insights into the relationship between truth and everything that exists. While he is always careful to be faithful to Scripture, Poythress demonstrates once again his remarkable capacity for creative thinking."

Wayne Grudem, Distinguished Research Professor of Theology and Biblical Studies, Phoenix Seminary

Truth, Theology, and Perspective

Crossway Books by Vern S. Poythress

Truth, Theology, and Perspective

An Approach to Understanding Biblical Doctrine

Vern S. Poythress

:: CROSSWAY®

WHEATON, ILLINOIS

Truth, Theology, and Perspective: An Approach to Understanding Biblical Doctrine

Copyright © 2022 by Vern S. Poythress

Published by Crossway
        1300 Crescent Street
        Wheaton, Illinois 60187

Cover design: Spencer Fuller, Faceout Studios

Cover image: Shutterstock

First printing 2022

Printed in the United States of America

Trade paperback ISBN: 978-1-4335-8024-6
ePub ISBN: 978-1-4335-8027-7
PDF ISBN: 978-1-4335-8025-3
Mobipocket ISBN: 978-1-4335-8026-0

Library of Congress Cataloging-in-Publication Data

Names: Poythress, Vern S., author.
Title: Truth, theology, and perspective : an approach to understanding biblical doctrine / Vern S. Poythress.
Description: Wheaton, Illinois : Crossway, 2022. | Includes bibliographical references and index.
Identifiers: LCCN 2021040800 (print) | LCCN 2021040801 (ebook) | ISBN 9781433580246 (trade paperback) | ISBN 9781433580253 (pdf) | ISBN 9781433580260 (mobi) | ISBN 9781433580277 (epub)
Subjects: LCSH: Theology, Doctrinal. | Bible—Hermeneutics. | Truth—Religious aspects—Christianity.
Classification: LCC BT75.3 .P69 2022 (print) | LCC BT75.3 (ebook) | DDC 230/.041—dc23
LC record available at https://lccn.loc.gov/2021040800
LC ebook record available at https://lccn.loc.gov/2021040801

Crossway is a publishing ministry of Good News Publishers.

VP			31	30	29	28	27	26	25	24	23	22
15	14	13	12	11	10	9	8	7	6	5	4	3	2	1

Contents

To John Frame, who taught me about perspectives

Introduction: Truth as a Perspective

IN THIS BOOK we use the theme of *truth* as one perspective by which to explore the riches of biblical teaching. It is not the only possible starting point, but it is one.

The Goal of the Book

We should explain a little bit about what we intend to do. We do not intend to *add* to biblical teaching or to the major doctrines already taught in the best books on systematic theology. Nor will we focus on *establishing* what the Bible teaches by surveying a large number of biblical passages on each topic and then developing extensive arguments based on these passages. Rather, we will be repeating what is found already in the Bible itself, in various passages. In addition, we will be repeating what is found in textbooks of systematic theology. What is new is that we will be using the theme of *truth* as a primary perspective on all these teachings.

By using truth as a perspective, we hope to encourage readers to appreciate more deeply the beauty of biblical teaching and its inner harmony. Any one aspect of doctrine, such as the theme that God is true and that the Bible is true, is in harmony with every other aspect.

Starting Assumptions

We should make clear at the beginning two convictions.

First, we should be convinced from the Bible that the Bible is itself the word of God. It is true and reliable in all that it affirms, with the reliability and truthfulness of God himself. Therefore, in the Bible we have a firm source for knowing the truth about matters that the Bible addresses.[1]

Second, the explanations of the Bible in this book are in harmony with what is known as Reformed theology, as summarized in the Reformed creeds.[2] This book represents that kind of theology, rather than other streams of theology that disagree on some important points. Given the goal of this book, we will not be focusing on the disagreements but rather on the positive explanation of biblical teaching.

Using a Perspective

In discussing biblical teaching, we will be using a *perspective*, namely the perspective that starts with the theme of truth. This kind of use of perspective differs radically from the ideas sometimes found in post-

---

1 For confirmation of the divine authority of the Bible, readers may consult a number of excellent books expounding its authority. See, in particular, Benjamin B. Warfield, *The Inspiration and Authority of the Bible* (Philadelphia: Presbyterian & Reformed, 1948); and John M. Frame, *The Doctrine of the Word of God* (Phillipsburg, NJ: P&R, 2010). For questions of how to interpret the Bible, readers may consult Vern S. Poythress, *God-Centered Biblical Interpretation* (Phillipsburg, NJ: P&R, 1999); and Vern S. Poythress, *Reading the Word of God in the Presence of God: A Handbook for Biblical Interpretation* (Wheaton, IL: Crossway, 2016).

2 See, for example, https://www.pcaac.org/bco/westminster-confession/, accessed June 1, 2020. Westminster Theological Seminary and the conservative Presbyterian churches in the United States allow that its teachers may take exception to individual points in the confessional standards, but they must agree with the overall system of doctrine. See also the Three Forms of Unity, https://www.urcna.org/sysfiles/member/custom/custom.cfm?memberid=1651&customid=24288, accessed Feb. 2, 2021.

modern relativism. Relativism is skeptical about our ability to arrive at universal truth. But God speaks and makes known the truth, so a Christian believer should reject skepticism and relativism.

God is true and is true to himself. He speaks the truth in the Bible, which is his word. He displays who he is in the things that he has made (Rom. 1:18–23). He sends the Holy Spirit to renew our hearts, so that we may know the truth (Eph. 1:17–18). These realities about God imply that we have a firm basis for confidence in what we come to know as we read the Bible.[3] Believers may, of course, still be mistaken on some points of doctrine. The existence of the Bible, and the gift of the Holy Spirit, do not make us infallible. But on central points of biblical teaching, we may come to a confident understanding of the truth. The Bible is clear in its central points, and the Holy Spirit is sent out by God to remove obstacles from the hearts of those who belong to him.[4]

With this much explanation, we are ready to begin.

3　On perspectives, see John M. Frame, "A Primer on Perspectivalism," 2008, http://frame-poythress.org/a-primer-on-perspectivalism-revised-2008/, accessed Nov. 21, 2016; Vern S. Poythress, *Symphonic Theology: The Validity of Multiple Perspectives in Theology* (repr., Phillipsburg, NJ: P&R, 2001); Vern S. Poythress, *Knowing and the Trinity: How Perspectives in Human Knowledge Imitate the Trinity* (Phillipsburg, NJ: P&R, 2018).

4　The Westminster Confession of Faith 1.7 summarizes: "All things in Scripture are not alike plain in themselves, nor alike clear unto all: yet those things which are necessary to be known, believed, and observed for salvation, are so clearly propounded, and opened in some place of Scripture or other, that not only the learned, but the unlearned, in a due use of the ordinary means, may attain unto a sufficient understanding of them."

PART I

THE DOCTRINE OF GOD

1

The Existence of God

DOES GOD EXIST? The Bible says that he does (Genesis 1 and many other passages). The created world testifies that he exists (Rom. 1:18–23; Ps. 19:1–6). Even unbelievers know God (Rom. 1:21) but suppress this knowledge (v. 18). The miracles and fulfilled prophecies in the Bible confirm his existence. We can also consider an approach that confirms the existence of God by starting with the theme of truth.

What is truth? Truth is what God knows.[1] There is a close relation between the truth and God. So inspecting the idea of truth can actually confirm the existence of the true God, the one who knows all truth.

1   There is a little puzzle here, because, concerning anything that is false, God knows that it is false. So does God "know" all falsehoods? It depends on how we want to use the word *know*. I am using the word *know* in a fairly ordinary way. According to this usage, we can know something that is true. But we cannot know something that is false, that is, know it as true, because that is not knowledge at all, but mistaken belief.

   Let us illustrate: God knows that 2 + 2 = 4, but he does not know that 2 + 2 = 5. (To claim to know that 2 + 2 = 5 would be a mistake.) God also knows that it is false that 2 + 2 = 5. But what he knows is *not* that 2 + 2 = 5, but the affirmation, "It is false that 2 + 2 = 5."

THE DOCTRINE OF GOD

Truth Exists

Let us consider the claim that truth does not exist. This is an unusual claim, but something like it can be heard from some postmodernists, skeptics, and mystics.

But if truth does not exist, then it is true that truth does not exist. So, there is *something* that is true. Hence, the assumption that truth does not exist is self-refuting.

Truth exists. Not believing that it exists is self-defeating.

Attributes of Truth

Let us consider a particular example of a truth: $2 + 2 = 4$. This is true everywhere, throughout the universe. It is true at all times. Its truth does not change over time.[2]

So truth has three key attributes: omnipresence (everywhere present), everlastingness (through all times), and unchangeability (immutability). Unchangeability is actually stronger than the mere fact of no change. We are saying not only that truth does not change but that it *could* not change. These three features of truth are attributes of God. God is omnipresent, everlasting, and unchangeable. (See table 1.1.)

Table 1.1: Attributes of God and Attributes of Truth

God's Attributes	Attributes of Truth
omnipresence	omnipresence
everlastingness	everlastingness
unchangeability	unchangeability

2 For a similar exposition, see Vern S. Poythress, *Redeeming Science: A God-Centered Approach* (Wheaton, IL: Crossway, 2006), ch. 14.

Truth as Eternal

We can make a further, more refined point about everlastingness. God is not subject to time or captured by time. He is superior to time. So we may say that he is *eternal*.[3] The new heavens and the new earth, together with those who are redeemed in Christ, exist in the future without end, which means that they are *everlasting*. But they are still subject to time. God is different: he is superior to time; he is eternal. In addition, the truth that $2 + 2 = 4$ seems to be different. It is specified by God. As such, it is not subject to change with the passing of time.

Tensed Truths

In some ways, mathematical truths like $2 + 2 = 4$ are special, because they do not need to specify any one moment in time. Suppose, then, that we consider a truth that does have a time frame: Jesus Christ suffered under Pontius Pilate.[4] The name Pontius Pilate fixes the time frame as the first century. There is also an implicit geographical frame, namely the location of Jerusalem, where Pontius Pilate was ruling. The verb "suffered" accordingly is in the past tense, to indicate that the time at which the event occurred preceded the time in which we are now living.

There is a sense in which we might say that the truth about Jesus Christ suffering is not an "eternal" truth, but a *tensed* truth, a truth about a particular event. But notice that the truth about the event can be distinguished from the event itself. The event itself happened in the first century in Jerusalem, and is never to be repeated. We cannot see it directly before our eyes. But we can talk about whether it

3   Vern S. Poythress, *The Mystery of the Trinity: A Trinitarian Approach to the Attributes of God* (Phillipsburg, NJ: P&R, 2020), ch. 6.
4   Words from the Apostles' Creed.

happened. (It did.) The affirmation that it happened is an affirmation that continues to be true, through all future times.

What about past times? What about the times *before* Jesus Christ came into the world? At those earlier times, the event of Christ's crucifixion had not yet happened. But it was *planned* by God already:

> . . . you were ransomed from the futile ways inherited from your forefathers, not with perishable things such as silver or gold, but with the precious blood of Christ, like that of a lamb without blemish or spot. He was *foreknown before the foundation of the world* but was made manifest in the last times for the sake of you. (1 Pet. 1:18–20)

> . . . who saved us and called us to a holy calling, not because of our works but because of his own purpose and grace, which he gave us in Christ Jesus *before the ages began.* (2 Tim. 1:9)

> . . . for truly in this city there were gathered together against your holy servant Jesus, whom you anointed, both Herod and Pontius Pilate, along with the Gentiles and the peoples of Israel, to do whatever your hand and *your plan had predestined* to take place. (Acts 4:27–28)

Let us consider Acts 4:27–28 in more detail. The immediately preceding verses, Acts 4:25–26, cite Psalm 2, written a thousand years earlier, to confirm that the suffering and death of Christ were already planned by God. So a thousand years earlier it was already infallibly true, according to the plan of God, that Christ would suffer under Pontius Pilate *when the time came* for the events to take place. The truth about what took place was already true in God's sovereign plan. The truth is distinct from the events that it describes.

What about other, less significant truths? Second Kings 22:1 says that "Josiah was eight years old when he began to reign." No passage of the Bible indicates explicitly that this coronation of an eight-year-old was planned beforehand before God. But the Bible does give us a general principle, that God has planned all of history, including its details: "[God] works *all things* according to the counsel of his will" (Eph. 1:11; see Ps. 139:16). So the same principle holds for minor truths. Every truth is omnipresent, eternal, and unchangeable.

We see impressive illustrations of the unchangeable nature of truth when God fulfills his prophetic word. Consider, for example, the special prophecy in 1 Kings 13:2 about Jeroboam's altar: "Behold, a son shall be born to the house of David, Josiah by name, and he shall sacrifice on you [the altar] the priests of the high places who make offerings on you, and human bones shall be burned on you." This prophecy was proclaimed by an unnamed prophet in the presence of Jeroboam (v. 1), the first king in the northern kingdom of Israel, after the split between the northern and southern kingdoms (12:20). It was fulfilled hundreds of years later: "And as Josiah turned, he saw the tombs there on the mount. And he sent and took the bones out of the tombs and burned them on the altar . . ." (2 Kings 23:16). This truth about the judgment on Jeroboam remains true forever.

We could multiply cases like this. The prophet Micah predicted that Jesus the Messiah would be born in Bethlehem (Mic. 5:2). The prediction took place in the eighth century BC (1:1), hundreds of years before Jesus was born in Bethlehem (Matt. 2:1–6). Predictions like these confirm that God has an unchanging plan. The truths about this plan do not change. They cannot change.

Other Attributes of Truth

Other characteristics of truth match characteristics traditionally associated with God:

Truth is true. Likewise God is true.

Truth is *invisible*, though the things about which it speaks may be visible.

Truth is *immaterial*. That is, it is not a material thing like an orange, made out of atoms and with a particular location in space. Some truths are truths *about* material things. But the truths themselves can be distinguished from the things about which they speak.

Now let us consider two attributes of God together: *transcendence* and *immanence*. Do truths display both transcendence and immanence? It is easier to see that they do if we consider truths that apply to more than one case. For example, it is true that $2 + 2 = 4$. This truth applies to many instances, in which 2 apples plus 2 apples equals 4 apples, or 2 oranges plus 2 oranges equals 4 oranges. Truths that apply to more than one case *transcend* the world about which they speak. They transcend the particular cases. At the same time, truth is *immanent*, in the sense that it has bearing on particular cases. Transcendence and immanence are both attributes of truth. They are also attributes of God.

What about truths that are focused only on a particular case? Consider this truth: "Josiah was eight years old when he began to reign" (2 Kings 22:1). It deals with only one case, namely Josiah, at one time, namely when he began to reign. But even here, because the truth is true forever, it transcends the moment at which Josiah began to reign.

Truth is *infinite* in the sense that any one truth comes together with an infinite number of other truths. As an example, consider again the truth that $2 + 2 = 4$. It implies any number of other truths:

$2 + 2 = 4$.

It is true that $2 + 2 = 4$.

It is true that [it is true that $2 + 2 = 4$].

It is true that [it is true that [it is true that $2 + 2 = 4$]].

It is true that [it is true that [it is true that [it is true that $2 + 2 = 4$]]].

It is true that [it is true that [it is true that [it is true that [it is true that $2 + 2 = 4$]]]].

. . .

None of these truths simply repeats any of the truths on the preceding lines. So truth is infinite.

This particular example, of multiplying truths, might seem to be contrived. We are multiplying words. But we are not really changing anything about the world. Are we really adding anything significant when we add a truth that comments on the truth of the previous line?

It is true that we have not changed the world. Nor have we changed what is true about the world. But we have shown that there are an infinite number of truths. It is one way in which we may look into the infinite depths in God, which are also depths in the mind of God.

The addition of the expression "it is true that" may look like a contrivance. But if we start asking how it is possible to do such a thing, it opens up some profundities about language and about the human mind. A piece of language can talk about another piece of language. And this capability in language corresponds to a capability in the human mind. We can stand back from what we have already done, or what we have already thought, and try to see the whole scene again, from our "stand back" position. It is a way in which we are able to "transcend" the immediacy of our situation and the immediacy of our actions. We can *reflect* on the situation. And then we can reflect on our reflections, and so on. This "transcendence," so-called, is not the transcendence of God. But it is *imitative* of God's transcendence. We are in effect imagining how to look down on a situation from a higher viewpoint. And the highest viewpoint of all is God's. We are thinking God's thoughts after him, though we are still doing it on the level of being a creature.[5]

In addition, truth is morally *absolute*. It makes an absolute claim on us to give it our allegiance. For example, it is true that the law of gravity implies that if you leap off a tall building, you will fall to the ground. Someone may struggle against this truth. He may wish that it were not so. He may wish that he could fly just by willing himself to fly. He may be deluded and think that he has superhuman powers. But all his wishing and thinking and willing do not negate the claim of the truth on him. If he ignores the claim, he will fall to his death.

Not every truth has such a dramatic impact. But every truth makes a claim. And everyone who ignores truth puts himself in danger.

Is Truth Personal?

People who do not want to believe in a personal God might try to escape such belief by imagining that individual truths, or the whole body of all truth, are just out there as an impersonal abstraction. But this alternative is not plausible. Truth is rational. Rationality belongs to persons, but not to rocks. Truth is language-like (even before we

5 Vern S. Poythress, *Logic: A God-Centered Approach to the Foundation of Western Thought* (Wheaton, IL: Crossway, 2013), ch. 45; Vern S. Poythress, *Redeeming Mathematics: A God-Centered Approach* (Wheaton, IL: Crossway, 2015), ch. 8; Vern S. Poythress, "The Quest for Wisdom," in *Resurrection and Eschatology: Theology in Service of the Church: Essays in Honor of Richard B. Gaffin, Jr.*, 86–114, ed. Lane G. Tipton and Jeffrey C. Waddington (Phillipsburg, NJ: P&R, 2008), https://frame-poythress.org/the-quest-for-wisdom/.

express a truth in a particular human language). The complexity of many truths illustrates a complexity of language surpassing the signaling that takes place among animals. Language ability—of the complexity needed for dealing with truth—belongs to persons.

Truth and God

Truth has the attributes of the God of the Bible. These attributes include the fact that God is personal. Truth is another name for God. In fact, the Bible confirms this reality. Christ tells us that "I am the way, and the *truth*, and the life" (John 14:6). John 3:33 says that "God is true." We are accustomed to moving in our thought from God to the truths that God knows. Because God exists, truth exists. But we can move in the reverse direction. Since truth exists, God exists, because God is the truth.

We need to add that these affirmations do not imply that truth is something *behind* God, something more ultimate than God. God is "the last thing back," so to speak. He is the most ultimate origin.[6] So truth exists in him, not "in back of him," as if it were something outside of God to which he is forced to conform.

We may appeal at this point to the doctrine of divine *simplicity.* "Simplicity" is used here as a technical term in theology. It does not mean that God is "simple" for us to understand. Rather, it means that he is not made up of parts into which he could be divided. He is "simple" in contrast to being *composite.* Consider an example. A pencil is a composite item, since it can be divided up into the lead, the wooden shaft, and the eraser. Since God is immaterial, it is impossible to divide him up into material parts. But it is also impossible to

6   Vern S. Poythress, *The Mystery of the Trinity: A Trinitarian Approach to the Attributes of God* (Phillipsburg, NJ: P&R, 2020), ch. 3.

THE DOCTRINE OF GOD

divide him up *conceptually*, into abstract concepts that would precede him and subject him to their requirements. Truth is an example of one such concept. Truth is not more ultimate than God. Rather, it is a way in which God is.[7]

An Application

Since every truth reveals God, we can be confident in talking about God to unbelievers. Frequently, they do not acknowledge God's presence in their lives. But he is there. They rely on him. As Romans 1:21 reminds us, they "know" God, but they suppress that knowledge. They know God even in the process of saying anything that is true. The challenge for us is not to speak into a situation of complete ignorance, but to speak about God and his redemption in Christ. And then we pray that God may send the Holy Spirit to change their hearts. May he use our speech, our expressions of truths, in bringing unbelievers to faith.

For ourselves, the display of God in truth should stimulate thankfulness. Every truth that we know derives from God, who is glorious in his omnipresence, his eternality, and his unchangeability.

---

7   Poythress, *Mystery of the Trinity*, ch. 9.

2

Attributes of God

WE MAY CONTINUE by seeing how various attributes of God are displayed in his truthfulness. "Attributes" of God are terms describing who he is. He is *eternal, infinite, transcendent, good, loving,* and so on. When we consider God's truthfulness, we can see that it goes together with many other attributes. His attributes are on display *in* his truthfulness.

There is an underlying general principle here, related to simplicity. As we have seen, divine simplicity means that God cannot be divided up. Subordinately, it implies that his attributes cannot be divided up, so that we could place distinct attributes into neatly separated bins. We cannot cut out one attribute at a time, and consider it in *isolation* from everything else that God is. In fact, each attribute describes the whole of God, not just a part of him. If so, it also describes every *other* attribute, because all the attributes belong to who God is.

Truth is one attribute of God. So in this attribute it ought to be possible to see the other attributes, all of which belong to truth.

Simplicity

Let us begin with simplicity. Each attribute corresponds to some truth about God. It is true that God is omnipresent (everywhere present). It is true that God is eternal. It is true that God is unchangeable. Each of these truths is in the environment of the others. We cannot have one without the others. If by *attributes* we mean permanent features of God's character, they all belong together, because they all belong to the one God. This inherent "belonging together" is another way of describing *simplicity.* It is equivalent to saying that God is simple. Or, because we are using the attribute of truth, we may say that truth is simple. That does not mean that there is only one formulation of truth. But it does mean that all the formulations belong together, each formulation having the attributes of God and belonging to the unity that is in God.

We may see one effect of this unity if we reflect on the fact that no truth can be thought about or discussed in total isolation from everything else. For example, for it to be meaningful to say, "God is omnipresent," we have to have a sense of what it means to be present. And within the created world, his presence is a presence everywhere in *space.*

Omniscience

The next attribute is *omniscience.* God knows all things. We have said that God is truth. So he is *all truths* together. Since he is personal, he knows himself, and knows all truths. For example, he knew everything about David while David was still in the womb: "For you formed my inward parts; you knitted me together in my mother's womb" (Ps. 139:13). He knows the words that we will speak before we speak them: "Even before a word is on my tongue, behold, O LORD, you know it altogether" (v. 4).

Absoluteness

God is *absolute*. By this we mean that he is not dependent on anything outside himself. This attribute is closely related to simplicity. There is nothing in back of God on which he might be dependent. We can confirm this attribute if we think about the way in which we experience contact with the truth. We are dependent on the truth. It makes an absolute claim on us.

We might think that at least *some* truths are dependent on the world. Consider a particular case: Oak trees, like other trees, reproduce according to their kind (Gen. 1:11–12). That is a truth about oak trees. Naively, it might appear that this truth depends on the *prior* fact that oak trees exist in the world. So is *this* truth dependent on the world? To be sure, it is a truth *about* the world. And we as human beings do come to know about it because of God's word in Genesis 1:11–12 and also because there are oak trees that we can observe. But what is the *origin* of the truth? The origin is in God, not in the world.

As we saw in thinking about the eternity of truth, truth exists even before the world existed. God had a plan (Isa. 46:9–10; Eph. 1:11) for the world. In his plan, he knew beforehand everything that would take place. So he also knew all truths. The truths about oak trees *precede* the oak trees. The oak trees are dependent on the truths, rather than the reverse.

Omnipotence

The fact that the truth about various things precedes the things in the world has other implications. It means that the things in the world are held by the truth about them, rather than the truth being held as an idea subordinate to the world. When we focus on human knowledge, there are respects in which our knowledge is subordinate to the world, because we have to find out about the world. For example, I know that there is an oak tree in my front yard because the oak tree is there. The oak tree precedes my knowledge about it. But God's knowledge is different. God's knowledge about the oak tree precedes the oak tree. God planned for the oak tree to be there. That is why it is there. So truth in the mind of God precedes the oak tree.

So, in thinking about truth, we affirm aspects about how God governs the world. We are finding out about God, not merely about the world. Any truth about the world that we find is a truth that exists in God. So the world is subordinate in this way to the truth.

Truth, then, is omnipotent. The world is always, everywhere, thoroughly and perfectly subordinate to the truths in God:

> all the inhabitants of the earth are accounted as nothing,
>   and he does according to his will among the host of heaven
>   and among the inhabitants of the earth;
> and none can stay his hand
>   or say to him, "What have you done?" (Dan. 4:35)

> Who has spoken and it came to pass,
>   unless the Lord has commanded it?
> Is it not from the mouth of the Most High
>   that good and bad come? (Lam. 3:37–38)

Goodness

Though there may be some truths that we evade at first, we find that, at a foundational level, truth is good. And it is good for us. If we have mistaken ideas about truth, we have mistaken ideas about the world. And these mistaken ideas may lead to disaster.

We may consider again a simple example. We cannot fly through the air and defy the law of gravity just by wishing we could. If we do not know this truth, we may imagine that we can fly through the air, and we injure ourselves by trying. It is *good* to know that we cannot will ourselves to fly through the air, because it protects us from disaster. It also protects us from disappointment.

It is *good* that there is an oak tree in my front yard. It is good because God creates good things. The oak tree is good. And it is good because the oak tree can be an occasion for me to admire God and praise him for what he has made.

Since God is a God of truth, God is *good.*

The Will of God

If God is good, God also *wills* what is good. He desires what is good. So he approves of the truth. The truth is what God wills. God's having a will is one of his attributes. We may once again use the oak tree as an example. The oak tree is there because it was part of the truths in God's plan that he planned for the oak tree to be there. He also *willed* it to be there. He desired it to be there.

Mercy

In our fallen condition, in rebellion against God, we do not deserve to receive the truth. So when truth comes to us, it comes as a mercy. The fact that we have some truth at all reflects the fact that God is *merciful.* People in rebellion against God can become so confused that they doubt the existence of the world. They might think that the oak tree in my front yard is only an illusion of an oak tree. God has rescued me from this delusion in giving me a conviction that the oak tree is there. Though sane people tend to take for granted such truths about the world, those truths are a gift. Each of us could have been insane.

Love

We know deep down that the proper response to the truth is to love it. This should be taking place in the level of humanity, in our human response. But because we are made in the image of God, our human response reflects on the creaturely level something about God. What is God's natural relation to the truth? God is *loving*, and he loves the truth.

Righteousness

Each particular truth, such as $2 + 2 = 4$, fits the facts. When we come to the moral dimensions of personal action, this sense of "fitness" includes the fit *evaluation* of human persons, acts, and attitudes. "Righteousness" is moral fitness. Righteousness in the setting of a human court may also include attention to punishments for wrongdoing. The punishment has to *fit* the crime. "As you have done, it shall be done to you; your deeds shall return on your own head" (Obad. 15).[1] Righteousness is the *truth* about the evaluation of moral acts. God is a God of truth. So he is also a God of righteousness. "Righteous are you, O Lord, and right are your rules" (Ps. 119:137).

Holiness

Holiness is closely related to moral absoluteness, which we mentioned above. Truths make absolute moral claims on us. And by transcending

---

1 Vern S. Poythress, *The Shadow of Christ in the Law of Moses* (1991; repr., Phillipsburg, NJ: P&R, 1995), ch. 9.

us, they show that they have the holiness of God. Consider a comparison. The living creatures in Revelation 4 stand in the presence of God. They are holy, reflecting the holiness of God. Truths are in a sense even more in the presence of God, because they are in his mind. They are therefore holy. They manifest the exalted purity of God.

We may look at it another way. Truth is by nature not contaminated with error. Truth may be mixed with error in our own minds and our apprehensions. But truth itself is true and not erroneous. It is uncontaminated. That is to say, it is pure. *Holiness* is the word to describe the perfect purity of God. The truth about the oak tree in my front yard is pure, within God's mind. The oak tree in this respect displays the holiness of God.

An Application

The attributes of God displayed in the truth are glorious. The fitting response is to praise God and to serve him. You may ask what truths God has brought to your attention today, and how they display his glory.

3

The Trinity

NEXT WE CONSIDER the doctrine of the Trinity.

Affirming the Mystery

The doctrine of the Trinity says that there is only one true God, and also that this one God is three persons. The three persons are the Father, the Son, and the Holy Spirit. Each person is fully God.

The doctrine of the Trinity is deeply mysterious. God is not equal to anything in the world that he has made. There is no model within the world that captures everything about him.

As with the preceding chapters, our purpose is not to *establish* the doctrine of the Trinity. To do that, we would have to give an extensive discussion of particular biblical texts.[1] Rather, we consider that it is already established. The doctrine of the Trinity is a distillation of what many Bible texts say about God, confirmed by many arguments offered through the course of church history. Our purpose, then, is to confirm the harmony of this doctrine using our starting theme, the theme of truth.

---

1 Vern S. Poythress, *Knowing and the Trinity: How Perspectives in Human Knowledge Imitate the Trinity* (Phillipsburg, NJ: P&R, 2018), ch. 6.

The Truth and Its Subject Matter

Earlier we considered truths about the created world. We saw that the truth precedes the things about which the truth speaks. For example, the truth about oak trees precedes the oak trees. But now consider truths about God, such as the truth that God is good. If we say that this truth precedes God, we get into trouble. The doctrine of simplicity and the doctrine of God's absoluteness say that nothing precedes God. Goodness goes back as far as God goes, but it does not "precede" him. Nor does God precede goodness, if what we mean is that God initially exists, and then at some later point he decides to become good or takes on goodness as an extra attribute. No. God is *necessarily* good.

In all this, it is still possible to make a *distinction* between God and the truth that God is good. We can distinguish two meanings. We distinguish, but we cannot separate.

Since God is absolute, he has resources in himself for this distinction. God is one God, one in his simplicity. But there is also a diversity. There is a distinction between God and the truth of God. This truth of God is in the Bible called "the Word" and the truth (John 1:1; 14:6). God is one God. But there are also distinct persons. There is God the Father, who preeminently represents God (such as in the first part of John 1:1 and in Gal. 4:4; Heb. 1:2). There is God the Son, who is the Word and the expression of the Father. There is also the Holy Spirit, who conveys the truth to us.

In addition, it seems there is a kind of logical order, or order in thought, when we consider truths about God. Truths about God express who God is. The expression exists in God already, but there is a sense of movement from God to expression. This sense of movement has its root in the eternal begetting of the Son by the Father. In addition, the Holy Spirit proceeds from the Father and the Son.

God Speaking

We have said that God is personal. One of the fundamental features about being personal is communication. Complex communication takes place using the wonderful complexity of language. Since God is personal, he is a communicator. This feature holds true even apart from God's creating the world. He does not need the world (he is absolute). So there is communication within God. We have said that the truth is expressed. We might alternatively say that it is communicated. This communication involves a differentiation. There is God the communicator; and then there is the communication itself. And there is God the hearer or receiver, as indicated in John 16:13. So there is a triad in communication, consisting of (1) the communicator, who originates the communication; (2) the communication itself; and (3) the receiver of the communication. This triad has been discussed elsewhere as a reflection of the Trinity.[2] The preeminent communicator is designated the Father. The communication itself is the Son, who is called the Word (John 1:1). In one passage, the Holy Spirit is the hearer of divine speech:

> When the Spirit of truth comes, he will guide you into all the truth, for he will not speak on his own authority, but *whatever he hears* he will speak, and he will declare to you the things that are to come. (John 16:13)

The Holy Spirit is also sometimes represented as like the breath of God bearing the word to its goal (Ezek. 37:9–14).

There is a natural order in the communication of God. The communication goes from the Father, and issues in the Son, whom the Holy Spirit hears, according to John 16:13. The going of the Son as the Word is an alternative analogy to describe the eternal begetting of the Son.

2 Poythress, *Knowing and the Trinity*, ch. 8.

The Son is the Truth. As the Truth, he expresses the Father. The Father, the Son, and the Holy Spirit share in all the classical attributes of God, as implied by the doctrine of simplicity, which affirms the inseparability of one attribute from others. The fact of differentiation among the persons goes mysteriously together with the commonality of attributes. (Classically, the commonality is stated as "one essence," meaning that there is only one God, and that each person is fully God; each person has all the attributes of God.)

Truth Implying Love

We also saw earlier that truth naturally evokes love. One implication is that the Father loves the Son, as indeed it says in John 3:35 and 5:20. Or we may prefer to start with the truth that God is personal. One of the prime features of persons is that they can love. We infer that God loves. Love is *inter*personal. It implies a lover, a loved one, and the love between them. This triad holds true with respect to God. According to John 3:35 and 5:20, the Father is the lover, the Son is the loved one, and the Holy Spirit is closely associated with the love between them, according to John 3:34–35.[3] The terms *Father* and *Son* indicate that the love among persons in the Trinity is the archetype, or original pattern, that is imitated by the human love of a father for his son.

Truth Implying Reflections

The truth expressed in the Word of God reflects who the Father is. In fact, the reflection is an exact reflection: "He [the Son] is the radiance of the glory of God and the *exact imprint* of his nature" (Heb. 1:3).

3 Poythress, *Knowing and the Trinity*, 317–18, imitating Augustine, "On the Holy Trinity," in *Nicene and Post-Nicene Fathers*, 1st. series, ed. Philip Schaff (London: T & T Clark, 1980), 3:124 (8.10); 3:215–17 (15.17).

Thus, the idea of truth contains within it also the idea of reflection. Truth reflects what is real.

The Son is also called "the image of the invisible God" (Col. 1:15). Thus, when we think about truth in God, we are led naturally to see a differentiation among the persons. God the Father is the archetype; God the Son is the image. The Son is also the truth of God (John 14:6). It is not immediately clear how the Holy Spirit fits in, but in various places in the Bible, the Holy Spirit is closely associated with the glory of God in theophany (1 Pet. 4:14). Old Testament theophanies anticipate the appearing of the Son of God in the flesh. In theophanies, the Father is the archetype. He is displayed in an image, such as in Ezekiel 1:26–28. The image corresponds to the Son. It is the Son of God who appears in human form in Ezekiel 1:26–28.

We can see this truth if we compare Ezekiel 1:26–28 with Revelation 1:12–16. In Revelation 1:12–16, Jesus appears to John in a revelation of the glory of God. Some of the features in Revelation 1:12–16 are similar to what is found in Ezekiel 1:26–28. For example, the "human" appearance in Ezekiel 1:26 corresponds to the human form that Jesus has in Revelation 1:12–16. The fire and gleaming metal in Ezekiel 1:27 correspond to the eyes "like a flame of fire" in Revelation 1:14 and the "burnished bronze" in verse 15. The brightness in Ezekiel 1:27 corresponds to "the sun shining in full strength" in Revelation 1:16. The glory of God is the glory of the Father expressed in the Son and serves as a kind of bond in the Spirit between the archetype and its reflection.[4]

The pattern of an archetype and its reflection reinforces what we observed earlier about God's attribute of justice. The sense of "fitness" that we see in justice is similar to the fitness in the way in which the

4 Poythress, *Knowing and the Trinity*, ch. 8.

truth matches the subject matter and matches any expressions of the truth. The match means that the truth fits the subject matter that it describes. Because of the similarity between righteousness and truth, we might say that righteousness *reflects* truth. Or we could go in the other direction, and say that truth reflects righteousness.

Three Analogies for the Trinity

Thus, reflection on the nature of truth has led us to see that the nature of truth is in harmony with the Trinity. More specifically, it has led us to reaffirm the three primary analogies that the Bible itself uses in describing the distinctions between two persons of the Trinity. These analogies are the analogy with communication (the Son as the Word; John 1:1; and the Holy Spirit as the breath of God; Ezek. 37:10, 14), the analogy with a family (the second person of the Trinity as Son), and the analogy with reflections (the Son as Image).[5] Each of these takes place in the truth. The analogy with communication is an analogy in which the truth is communicated from the Father, who is the original communicator. The analogy with a family is also an analogy of love. The truth evokes love of the truth. And the analogy with reflections is illustrated by the truth reflecting what is (God himself).

In all three analogies, there is a movement representing the order of persons in the Trinity. God speaks the Word; the Father begets the Son; and God the Father reflects himself in the Image. The Holy Spirit serves respectively as hearer or breath, as the bond of love, and as the glory between archetype and image. Or we may say that the Father communicates the Truth, which the Holy Spirit receives. (The Spirit *also* communicates truth to us, as John 16:13 affirms.)

5 Poythress, *Knowing and the Trinity*, ch. 8.

Coinherence of Persons of the Trinity

Finally, we should mention briefly the doctrine of coinherence. *Coinherence* is one of the terms used to describe the fact that each person of the Trinity indwells each other person. We may say that the persons "coinhere." This truth is indicated in John 17:21, 23, and in John 14:23. This teaching is clearest when we turn to the specific passages that say that the Father dwells in the Son and the Son dwells in the Father. But it is also an implication of what we have observed about the truth. Each person of the Trinity knows the truth exhaustively. Each person knows the other persons completely. And if God is truth, knowing the truth in divine fullness implies dwelling in God, and therefore dwelling in each distinct person of the Trinity.

Coinherence also implies that each person of the Trinity acts *with* the other persons. None acts independently, because they are indwelt by the other persons. The situation is analogous to the fact that, if the Holy Spirit dwells in us and is at work in us, we do not act independently. We do act, but also God acts in us: "it is God who works in you, both to will and to work for his good pleasure" (Phil. 2:13).[6]

An Application

Coinherence leads us to praise God. He dwells in those who trust in Christ. That indwelling blesses us and empowers us. It is a reflection of the archetypal indwelling, namely the mutual indwelling of the persons of the Trinity.

We may also thank the Lord for the marvel of redemption. Our salvation takes place through the activities of all three persons of the Trinity. God the Father has planned redemption from before the

6   Poythress, *Knowing and the Trinity*, ch. 7.

foundation of the world (1 Pet. 1:20). Christ accomplished redemption through his life on earth, his death, his resurrection, and his ascension. The Holy Spirit applies redemption by coming to dwell in us. Each of these is a manifestation of the communion of persons, which is a communion in the truth.

4

The Plan of God

WHAT DOES THE NATURE OF TRUTH imply about God's plan for
the world?

God's Plan

We have already seen that truth exists in God even before events
take place in the world. The events that unfold in the world conform
to the truth about those events. The truth is already there because
God plans the history of the world comprehensively. His plan for
the oak tree in my front yard existed before the beginning of time.
Truth in God's mind goes together with a plan in God's mind. The
plan includes everything. God plans for the origin of each created
thing, including the oak tree. He sustains and guides each thing in
the course of its existence. And he plans its goal. The oak tree started
as an acorn, and God's goal for it was that it would grow into a mature
tree. Various verses all through the Bible indicate the comprehensiveness of God's involvement.[1] Ephesians 1:11 is particularly relevant:

---

1   Cf. Loraine Boettner, *The Reformed Doctrine of Predestination* (Grand Rapids,
    MI: Eerdmans, 1936); Vern S. Poythress, *Chance and the Sovereignty of God: A*

"... according to the purpose of him who works *all things* according to the counsel of his will." The plan of God is as comprehensive as the truth, and the truth that God knows includes all truth about all events of all times.

Human Agency

Sometimes people wonder about the question of human choice and human responsibility.[2] If God determines the future, are we still responsible? For example, I transplanted the oak tree in my front yard when it was still a sprout, less than a foot high. Did God determine beforehand that I would transplant it and put it where it now is? If he did, am I still responsible for having put it where it is?

We cannot in this book provide a full discussion. We will take up the topic briefly when we discuss human nature. For the moment, let us observe that our relationships to the truth can be of two kinds: we can respond, and we can initiate. In the first case, we respond to truths that we already know. In the second case, we take initiative and decide to act in the world, thereby bringing about new situations. And there are truths about these situations.

Let us take the oak tree as our example. Before I transplanted the oak tree, I knew passively that it was an oak tree. I also knew enough about trees to know that if I dug it up carefully, it would probably recover from the transplant and continue to grow in a new location. I knew certain truths by responding to what I saw about the oak tree in the world around me. Then I transplanted the tree. In the act of transplanting, I took the initiative. The oak tree sat at a new location

---

God-Centered Approach to Probability and Random Events (Wheaton, IL: Crossway, 2014), part 1.

2 Poythress, *Chance and the Sovereignty of God*, ch. 5.

because I decided to put it there. So there was response at one point and initiative at another point.

Let us consider these two kinds of relationships to truth.

In the first kind of relationship, we respond to truths. The truths can be truths about God such as he reveals in the Bible. Or we can respond to truths about our situation, which we come to know through ordinary observation. In such a case, it is clear that the truth already exists before we respond. We had no part in making the situation.

On the other hand, in the case of the second kind of relationship, we can in a sense *create* a new situation. I put the sprout of an oak tree in its new location. We say something new to a friend. Or we decide to take a new job. When we do such things, there are corresponding truths. There are truths about what we say. There are truths about the oak tree, namely that it is in its new location. There are truths about the new job. For example, we can properly say that it is true that we took the new job. These truths were unknown to human beings until the new situation came about (but they were known to God, and were part of his plan). If I eat my breakfast at 8:30 a.m. on June 3, it comes about that I am aware of a truth that is new to me, namely that I have eaten my breakfast at 8:30 a.m. on June 3.

Now, God is sovereign over both kinds of truth. As we have indicated, all truth originates in God. God is the Creator. He is greater than we are. But the Bible indicates that there are some analogies between God's personal activities and our human personal activities. So is there in God's activities a distinction between response and initiative?

We have to be careful. God never has to respond to a situation that is out of his control. If we use the word *respond* with respect to God, it does not mean what it means when human beings respond to situations out of their control.[3] God does respond, in answering the prayers of his people and in acting as judge to evaluate situations and people:

And after that God *responded* to the plea for the land. (2 Sam. 21:14)

And the dead were *judged* by what was written in the books, according to what they had done. (Rev. 20:12)

It is important to note, however, that God is not taken by surprise by human prayers and human situations. It is God who brings about these prayers and these situations, by his providential control, and in agreement with his plan.

God also creates new situations. It is this second part that shows most vividly the comprehensiveness of his rule. He rules everything:

The Lord has established his throne in the heavens,
and his kingdom rules over all. (Ps. 103:19)

Who has spoken and it came to pass,
unless the Lord has commanded it?
Is it not from the mouth of the Most High
that good and bad come? (Lam. 3:37–38)

The Bible pictures God as being like a king who issues *decrees*, commandments about his kingdom. The function of a king's decree is not to match a situation already out there, but to bring about a situation

3   Vern S. Poythress, *The Mystery of the Trinity: A Trinitarian Approach to the Attributes of God* (Phillipsburg, NJ: P&R, 2020), ch. 40.

specified in the decree. The king is able to bring it about because of the authority vested in him.

When God issues a command, he brings about a new situation in the world and all the truths involved in describing the situation. The truths are new, from the standpoint of human knowledge. But God knew them all along, because he already had a plan, even before he brought it about and made it known by bringing the new situation into existence.

So we may say that there are two kinds of truth. There are truths that are already true, within the plan of God, but are not yet known to human beings on the earth. Then there are truths that have become accessible to us on earth because God has brought about the situation specified by particular truths that express his plan. The distinction between the two kinds of truth arises because of the limits of human knowledge, not because of something innate in the quality of truth.

Truth and Necessity

Another distinction may be useful in thinking about truth. We can distinguish, at least roughly, between two categories of truth. On the one hand, there are truths having to do with who God always is; on the other hand, there are truths having to do with something he brings about in the world. Truths of the former kind are what we might call *necessary* truths. Truths of the latter kind are not necessary; they are *contingent.* A truth that is necessary could not have been otherwise. A truth that is contingent could have been different, if God had decided differently.

For example, that God is omniscient is a necessary truth. God is necessarily who he is. So also, it is necessary that God is good. On the other hand, that God created the world is a contingent truth. It is contingent because God is absolute. He has no needs. He did not *need* to create the world. He decided to do it. He also decided that my oak tree would grow into a mature tree in its new, rather than its old, location. He did not *need* to have that particular detail in his plan.

But did we not say earlier that truth is absolute? Any truth makes an absolute moral claim on us. But that is because it reflects the absoluteness of God, who specifies all truth and who knows all truth. But it still remains the case that not all truths are necessary.

Let us consider another kind of case. Suppose God makes known to us an aspect of his plan for the future, as he does in many instances of prophecy. For example, he promises that an offspring of the woman will crush the serpent (Gen. 3:15). He promises that the Messiah will arise from the line of David (Isa. 11:1–10). Once he makes known a part of his plan to us, we can be certain that this part of his plan will come to pass. We might say that it is *necessary.* That is, it is necessary, given the assumption that it is an aspect of God's plan. But the plan itself is not something necessary to who God is. As we saw, he did not have to create the world at all. And he did not have to create it in exactly the way he did. He did not have to make my oak tree.

There is mystery here. In the end, it goes back to the mystery of God's creativity. It is true that God is God, and that he is personal. As the personal God, he can make *choices.* Suppose we are considering some particular truth, such as the truth that "Josiah was eight years old when he began to reign" (2 Kings 22:1). This truth is one truth belonging to the overall plan of God, a plan from all eternity.

We intuitively sense two aspects to this truth. First, it transcends us. It exists eternally in the mind of God. Second, it could have been otherwise. (It is *contingent.*) It could have been that the new king had a name other than Josiah. (But given the prophecy about "Josiah" in 1 Kings 13:2, Josiah's name had to be Josiah. God could have planned for him to have another name; but then he would have had the prophecy in 1 Kings 13:2 provide this other name. God's plan is consistent.) It could have been that Josiah never existed—though, given God's promise to David, it was necessary that there be a line of kingly descendants leading to Christ, the final king in the line. It could have been that Josiah was nine or ten years old, rather than eight, when he began to reign. We can envision any number of possibilities. And, though we are not God and cannot directly inspect his mind, we sense that many of these possibilities were real possibilities for God too. God could have planned otherwise. He exercised his creativity and his ability to choose when he determined to have a world in which Josiah was eight years old when he began to reign.

God is ultimate, and therefore he is himself the ultimate resource behind all these possibilities. The differentiation in many possibilities must have its ultimate source in the prior differentiation in God himself.

It is all very mysterious. But we can begin with the truth that God is three persons. Moreover, the Father begets the Son, not in time, but in an eternal act. (Again, it is mysterious.) All the attributes of God belong to each of the persons: to the Father, to the Son, and to the Holy Spirit. But in the distinction between persons, some attributes are more obviously expressed in one rather than another. For example, the Bible indicates that the Father sends the Son into the world, and that the Son carries out the will of the Father (John 3:17; 5:30). The plan of God belongs preeminently to the Father. The plan is carried out by the Son. The plan is always the same. It is perfectly stable. The carrying out of the plan manifests preeminently the creativity of God, because new events take place.

We may accordingly associate the Father preeminently with the plan of God, and therefore also with the stability of God. The Son, as the one begotten, we may associate preeminently with the creativity of God.[4] Because there is an original or archetypal differentiation in God, there can also be a differentiation in possibilities and in what God does in acting in the world. We may put it another way. The original love is the love between the Father and the Son. This love expresses itself when God acts in the world. The original differentiation in God is reflected in differentiation in God's acts

This differentiation reflects itself also in the nature of truth. Truth is differentiated. There are many truths about many events in the world. Moreover, there are also what we might call "possible truths"—formulations that are not true in this world but which *might* have been true, had God chosen otherwise. And that also leads to further truths: it is true that it is possible, if God had planned otherwise, that Josiah could have been ten years old when he began to reign.

We can see rich wisdom in the very structure of truth. Remember the truths derivable from $2 + 2 = 4$:

$2 + 2 = 4$

It is true that $2 + 2 = 4$

It is true that [it is true that $2 + 2 = 4$]

It is true that [it is true that [it is true that $2 + 2 = 4$]]

. . .

$2 + 2 = 4$ "begets" other truths, in an unending sequence.

4 Poythress, *Mystery of the Trinity*, 58–60.

Creativity has its eternal archetype in God in the begetting of the Son. This creativity is then reflected in the way that one truth begets another, analogically speaking.

We can also illustrate using the example of my oak tree in my front yard:

There is an oak tree in my front yard

It is true that [there is an oak tree in my front yard]

It is true that [it is true that [there is an oak tree in my front yard]]

It is true that [it is true that [it is true that [there is an oak tree in my front yard]]]

An Application

We may thank God for *this* tree, *this* flower, *this* bird. We thank him for truths about these things, which could have been otherwise.

5

Creation

LET US TURN TO the doctrine of creation. *Creation* is God's act by which he brought into being the world and everything in it, as described in Genesis 1.

Plan and Act

God's plan to create the world existed eternally, before the foundation of the world (1 Pet. 1:20). Then the plan is executed in time. God creates, in accord with his plan.

We are looking at the doctrine of creation and other doctrines from the standpoint of the theme of truth. How is truth related to creation? There are several relations. Let us begin by considering God's creativity. Because God is creative, truths that God knows will also express and manifest his creativity. Some truths that we know are surprising. Some truths represent things that we could not have guessed beforehand. If I imagine myself to be an angel, thinking about how God might create the world, I would never have guessed that he would create an oak tree. I would not have guessed that he would create the particular oak tree that stands in my front yard.

The creativity that we sometimes see in truth is a reflection of the creativity that belongs to God. God is innately creative. It is because of his creativity that he created the world.

We may also focus on the truth that God created the world. This truth is there, in the plan of God, eternally. But when we contemplate this truth, we can see implications. One of the implications is that each act of creating something needs to be executed at the time that God has planned for that particular act.

For example, God first creates the heavens and the earth (Gen. 1:1). On the first day he creates light (v. 3). On the second day he creates the expanse that separates the waters (v. 6). On the third day he gathers the waters together and creates the plants (vv. 9, 11). And so on.

In each act of creation, we can see three phases. There is the plan, which is always there. Then there is the going out of the truth. This going out is a communication. God speaks. And then there is the obedience that responds to the command.

We see this kind of pattern repeatedly in Genesis 1:

Plan: plan to create light (presupposed in Gen. 1:3)
Going out: And God said, "Let there be light." (Gen. 1:3a)
Response: And there was light. (Gen. 1:3b)

Plan: plan to create dry land
Going out: And God said, "Let the waters under the heavens be gathered together into one place, and let the dry land appear." (Gen. 1:9a)
Response: And it was so. (Gen. 1:9b)

This pattern is summarized in Psalm 33:6, 9:

By the word of the LORD the heavens were made,
    and by the breath of his mouth all their host. . . .

For he spoke, and it came to be;
    he commanded, and it stood firm.

The archetype of communication of the truth is found in God himself. We saw this earlier when we introduced the analogy with communication. According to this analogy, the Father is the speaker; the Son is the Word; and the Holy Spirit functions as the breath bringing the word to its destination. This pattern is reflected when God speaks in order to create the world. God the Father is preeminently the speaker. It is implied that he has a plan to speak, even before he speaks. The Word, the second person of the Trinity, is expressed in the speech ("Let there be light," Gen. 1:3). The Holy Spirit is present, "hovering over the face of the waters" (Gen. 1:2). His immediate presence results in effects in the world. The word that God sends out is impressed on the things in the world.

This analogy is an analogy that involves the truth. It is truth that God has in his mind and that he speaks in the act of sending out his word.

Earlier, we talked about three main analogies that the Bible uses in describing distinctive relations among the persons of the Trinity. The first analogy, the analogy with communication, is close at hand when we see God speaking, as we do in Genesis 1. The second analogy, the analogy with a family, has bearing not only when we focus on the love of the Father for the Son, but also when we focus on activities of God impinging on the world. He created Adam and Eve as a family. The most outstanding activity in the whole history of the world is the accomplishment of redemption through Christ. In this accomplishment, the Father has planned. The Son is sent by the Father to accomplish the plan, to execute it in time and space. The Holy Spirit equips the Son for this work (Luke 3:22; 4:18). He also applies the work of Christ to those who believe. He is immediately present in their lives, by dwelling in them (Rom. 8:9–11). The family analogy, with the Father relating to the Son, is illustrated by God's redemptive actions in the world. In these actions, the Father is preeminently the planner; the Son is the executor or accomplisher; and the Holy Spirit works application.[1]

This pattern of action holds true in the case of God's work of creation. God the Father is preeminently the planner, and then also the speaker. God the Son, as the Word, expresses himself in the words of command from the Father, and executes the plan. God the Holy Spirit is present to apply the word to the things in creation (Gen. 1:2). As a result, "it was so." The created things conform to the command.

Creation from Nothing

One important point to make about creation is that God needs no preexisting material at the start. He creates out of nothing. "In the beginning, God created the heavens and the earth" (Gen. 1:1). Colossians 1:16 confirms that he made everything: "For by him all things were created, in heaven and on earth, visible and invisible, whether thrones or dominions or rulers or authorities—all things were created through him and for him." This lack of preexisting material underlines his complete sovereignty and control.

Creation out of nothing is in natural harmony with what we have seen about the truth. The truth in God's mind precedes everything

---

1 Vern S. Poythress, *Knowing and the Trinity: How Perspectives in Human Knowledge Imitate the Trinity* (Phillipsburg, NJ: P&R, 2018), 83–89.

in the world. The movement is from the truth to the things created, not the reverse. The truth itself is not already a "thing" separate from God. Rather, it is the contents of his mind, the contents of his plan. The truth has divine attributes, as we saw in chapter 1.

Creation with Purpose

The truth of God is comprehensive. God has all truth and knows all truth. He knows about the oak tree in my front yard. Likewise, the plan of God is comprehensive. It reaches from the beginning to the end (Rev. 1:8; 21:6; 22:13). The truths about creation include the purpose of creation. It displays the glory of God. Moreover, the pattern of six days of God's work, followed by a day of rest, includes an implicit allusion to the end. The end of God's work is his day of rest. Mankind, having completed its work, will enter into a final rest (Heb. 4:8–11), namely the new heavens and the new earth (Rev. 21:1).

Genesis 1–2 and Science

Because of the influence of modern science, people have questions about the relation of Genesis 1–2 to modern scientific accounts of the origin of the world, the origin of life, and the origin of mankind. We must refer people to other books for a more detailed discussion.[2] The unity of truth in the mind of God implies an ultimate unity and harmony between what the Bible says and what is true concerning the world. But human knowledge of the truth is limited, and affected by the fall into sin. Our interpretations of the Bible are fallible; and the work of scientists is fallible. Moreover, science in the twentieth century

---

2 Vern S. Poythress, *Redeeming Science: A God-Centered Approach* (Wheaton, IL: Crossway, 2006); Vern S. Poythress, *Interpreting Eden: A Guide to Faithfully Reading and Understanding Genesis 1–3* (Wheaton, IL: Crossway, 2019).

has become influenced by a view of the world that views the laws of science as impersonal rules, rather than as a human approximate account of the ways in which God personally rules the world. This impersonal view affects whether we believe that God can act exceptionally. He may have acted exceptionally at many points of origin, such as the origin of the universe as a whole, the origin of life, the origin of new kinds of animals, and, above all, in the origin of mankind.

An Application

Let us reckon with the fact that the truths about the world include the truth that each thing is made and that each thing has a particular purpose and contributes to God's overall goal, which is the display of his glory in the new heaven and the new earth. The oak tree is designed by God to manifest his glory. Let us praise God for his wisdom in his design.

6

Providence and Miracle

THE WORD *PROVIDENCE* is the customary term for designating God's continuing care for the world.

The Meaning of Providence

God's work of providence is a continuation of the care that he had when he made the world. The world as a whole has a plan behind it. The world also enjoys God's present-day rule over it, and God has his purposes for the future of the world. That is because the truths that specify the world are God's truths. They encompass a plan and a purpose.

Customarily, discussions of providence include three subdivisions: sustenance, concurrence (Latin, *concursus*), and governance.

First, there is *sustenance.* God *sustains* what he has already made. That is the aspect of truth looking to the past.

Second, there is *concurrence*, or "working with." God works in and with secondary causes in the present. (God is the *primary* cause of each event in the world. *Secondary* causes are causes operating between things in the world.) God's truth specifies not only what happens but *how* it happens. It specifies the links between events that are secondary causes. As usual, truth in the mind of God *precedes* the events that work out according to the truth. There can be no causal connections between various events in the world unless it is *true* that there are such causal connections. So the specification and control of God extend not only to the events but to the connections between various events in the world.

For example, the disasters that happen to Job, described in Job 1, all take place in a way that matches truths that are in God's eternal plan. Before the events happened, it was true already in God's plan that the Sabeans would "fall on" Job's oxen and donkeys (vv. 14–15). It was also true that the oxen and donkeys disappeared *because* the Sabeans took them. There was a causal sequence. The servants tending the oxen and donkeys died *because* the Sabeans "struck down the servants with the edge of the sword" (v. 15).

We can see here the operation of God as primary cause and also the genuine operation of secondary causes. As primary cause, God brought about the whole sequence. Job indicates that God did it all: "The LORD gave, and the LORD has taken away; blessed be the name of the LORD" (v. 21). At the same time, there were discernible secondary causes, such as the Sabeans and their swords. Job heard about them (vv. 14, 16, 17, 18). He does not deny that they exist; they are real. Satan was involved as well (1:12; 2:7).

Finally, the future is determined by God's purposes. *Governance* is the term for God's working *with purpose*, with a view to the goal in the future. Events are directed or *governed* toward that future.

Individual truths have a source in God. They have a meaning. And they have a purpose, God's purpose. So there are altogether three aspects to an individual truth: (1) the source; (2) the meaning; and (3) the purpose. These three aspects are related analogically to the three aspects of providence. The first aspect, sustenance, focuses on the relation of objects and events to their origin in the past. God sustains what he has already made in the past. The second aspect of providence, concurrence, focuses on God's work alongside secondary causes. He works in the present. This aspect is closely related to the meaning of the truth, which is there simultaneously with the truth. The third aspect of providence is governance, which focuses on purposes. Each event has purpose, which reflects the fact that each truth of God is related to God's purposes. In sum, in all three aspects, God's work in providence reflects the way in which truth functions.

We can once again illustrate using the oak tree in my front yard. God sustains the oak tree, once he has created it from the acorn. It continues to exist because God sustains its existence. With gradual alterations over time, it continues with the same shape and the same colors, because God sustains the tree. Second, God acts concurrently with secondary causes. The rain comes down. The sun shines on the leaves. Water and nourishing ingredients ascend from the roots to the tree. Chemical processes take place in the leaves. These are secondary causes. At one point, I myself become a secondary cause, when I dig up the tree and transplant it. All these secondary causes are real. God acts as primary cause *concurrently* with these secondary causes. We know he does, because the Bible teaches it. God affirms both primary and secondary causes in Job 1. We see both types of cause more specifically in Psalm 104:16:

> The trees of the LORD are watered abundantly,
>> the cedars of Lebanon that *he planted.*

So when I transplanted the oak tree, it was true that at the same time God was transplanting the tree. God worked concurrently with my work. I could not have done a single thing unless God was working concurrently. He was carrying out his eternal plan for the tree, in and through my work. This concurrence is wonderful and mysterious.

In an analogous way, God is present with the truth. The truth has meaning in the present. It expresses its own meaning, and simultaneously it is God's meaning.

Miracle

Miracles are extraordinary events that have special divine purposes and that evoke our awe and wonder. Some people think of miracles as violations of natural law. What do we think of this idea? Miracles violate our *expectations* about what will happen, and they may violate our approximations or best guesses about the regularities in the world. But they are within God's purposes. Truth can be surprising. And that shows that God can be surprising. And that shows that there can be miracles, which surprise us.

The nature of truth helps us to understand miracles. There are truths with respect to the regularities of the world. There are also truths with respect to what is extraordinary. Both kinds of events are equally derivative from God's plan, which encompasses all the truths about the world.

Some people worry that if we allow for the possibility of miracle, it would mean the end of predictability or even rationality. But God ordains the regularities in the world (as Gen. 1:11 reminds us) as well as events that for one reason or another are exceptional. As long as the exceptional is exceptional, we do not have chaos. And even the exceptional, we must remind ourselves, has a reason in the sight of God. For example, the resurrection of Christ is exceptional. Everyone, including the people who do not believe that it actually happened, recognize its exceptional character. But it is not irrational. The Bible explains the significance of the resurrection in God's purposes. God brought it about as the vindication and reward for Christ's obedience (Phil. 2:9–11). It is the basis for our new life and our own bodily resurrection (1 Cor. 15:44–49; Phil. 3:21; Col. 3:1–4). And so, without knowing everything about how Christ's resurrection happened, we can see how it harmonizes with the rest of God's purposes for the world.

In the same way, we can say that some truths are surprising or exceptional. They harmonize with truths that are less surprising, and truths that concern regular patterns in a larger number of events.

An Application

Understanding that miracles are not irrational gives us a basis for a more positive interest in miracles. It also encourages us to try to see what God's purposes are in any one particular miracle, and to ask what truths it puts on display. Miracles frequently underline truths about God that are displayed in providence. But these truths are displayed more spectacularly in miracles. For example, God cares for people and sometimes delivers them, even within this life, from bodily sicknesses (Pss. 103:3; 107:17–22). In providence, every healing that takes place in the whole history of the world displays God's power and kindness. Jesus's miracles of healing are spectacular instances of healing. They serve to authenticate his claims. But they also display in a vivid form what has been taking place when God heals providentially.

We may also observe that healing or other miracles depend entirely on God. No alleged system of natural regularities can prevent him from acting, if he chooses. So we are encouraged to pray that he will satisfy all our needs.

7

Revelation

LET US CONSIDER revelation in the light of the theme of truth. *Revelation* describes those acts of God in which he displays truth. The truths he shows are of many kinds. He shows himself, or something about his character, or some truth about the world, to people to whom he directs the revelation. He has shown me that there is an oak tree in my front yard.

Revelation in Relation to God

Revelation comes from God and reflects who God is. Revelation expresses the truth. So what we have seen about the relation of the truth to God is relevant to a consideration of revelation.

Revelation expresses God. So let us consider the analogy with communication. God is truth, and his truth comes to expression in the Son, who is the Word. The Father is the speaker and the Son is the Word who is spoken. This pattern manifests also the creativity of God.

God further manifests his creativity and love if he reveals something to the world or to human beings in the world. This creative expression reflects and expresses the archetypal creativity and expression of love in the eternal Word. Equally, we can say that revelation reflects God who is the truth, and God's revelation reveals truth. It expresses the truth already existing eternally in God.

Let us consider some examples. When God creates light, he displays on the level of the created order the fact that God is light (1 John 1:5). Created light is a reminder that God is pure, that he is good, and that he is the source for spiritual as well as physical illumination. He reveals truths about himself. Those truths about God were already true, but revelation conveys them to us.

In Genesis 3:15, God makes a verbal promise:

I will put enmity between you [the serpent] and the woman,
    and between your offspring and her offspring;
he shall bruise your head,
    and you shall bruise his heel.

This verbal communication reveals God and reveals truths about what will happen in the future of the world. It shows that God is merciful, because Adam and Eve deserved to die without having children. It shows that God is powerful, because he will bring about the victory over the serpent. When God actually accomplishes redemption through Christ, who is the "offspring" of the woman (Gal. 3:16), he shows that he is faithful. He shows his moral goodness in bringing an end to the evil introduced by the serpent. He also shows that Adam and Eve will have offspring, as Genesis 3:15 promises. All these truths were already true, but God's promise makes the truths accessible to the people who hear.

When God makes trees, the trees have a beauty to them. So, through them, God shows that he is beautiful. In a distant sense, every tree is a kind of reminder of the tree of life that was in the garden of Eden (Gen. 2:9; 3:22, 24). By being alive, and by giving us life-sustaining fruit or wood or other useful products, they testify to and reveal the goodness of God. They remind us that God is the living God, and that eternal life can be found only in him.

Modes of Revelation

Let us recall that there are three main analogies explicating the relations among the persons of the Trinity: the analogy with communication, the analogy with a family, and the analogy with reflections. These three reflect themselves in interlocking modes of revelation. Revelation can be verbal revelation, corresponding to the analogy with communication. Revelation can be ruling and caring revelation. This ruling and caring corresponds to ruling and caring that take place in a family. The analogy with a family is pertinent. Revelation can be revelation in presence, especially visible presence, as in theophanies. This mode of revelation corresponds more closely to the analogy with reflections.

We can also distinguish between special and general revelation, depending on who is the immediate recipient. Because God is himself the fullness of truth, he is capable of revealing truth either to one human being or to many. If he reveals truth to one person, or to a small number of people, we call it *special revelation*. If he reveals truth to the whole world (as he does through the sun, the moon, the stars, and the created order; Rom. 1:18–25), it is called *general revelation*.

God is true. His truth is true. So also, his revelation, both verbal and nonverbal, is true. There is no admixture of error.

We should add one important note: Work in natural science is the work of human beings, who expose themselves to general revelation.

The general revelation itself is true. But the scientists, as human beings, are not infallible in the way in which they receive and appreciate this revelation.[1]

The Bible

What is the status of the Bible? It would take a long detour to establish and confirm that the Bible is the word of God. We could point to many texts in the Bible. Other books have been written to do this job. For our purposes, we may be content with a short summary. Jesus says, "Your word is truth" (John 17:17). Earlier in the same chapter in John, Jesus indicates that his words are the words of God: "I have given them the words that you gave me" (v. 8). Jesus's words are true; indeed, he is the Truth (John 14:6). In John 10:35 Jesus indicates that the word of God came in Old Testament times. In Matthew 5:17 he indicates more indirectly that the law and the prophets are the word of God (compare Matt. 19:4–5). The apostles commissioned by Jesus continue with his authority.[2]

---

1 Vern S. Poythress, *Redeeming Science: A God-Centered Approach* (Wheaton, IL: Crossway, 2006), ch. 2.
2 I am aware that the historical-critical treatment of the Bible has become dominant in the universities of the modern West, and it raises doubts as to whether any of the passages above really represent the teaching of Jesus rather than merely the claims of human authors about what Jesus is alleged to have said. Discussing this point of view would lead to a long detour (cf. Vern S. Poythress, *Inerrancy and Worldview: Answering Modern Challenges to the Bible* [Wheaton, IL: Crossway, 2012]). Careful examination might show that this whole historical-critical tradition depends on truth. It uses truth, with its clear testimony to God, to deny truth. That is not a good starting point. It is better to be a disciple of Jesus. And we cannot be disciples of Jesus if we do not admit that he speaks to us. He does so in the Bible.

It is sad to have to be so negative about the state of the mainstream of the modern academic world. But we are not in a good state. We have abandoned the wisdom of God (Prov. 4:7).

The Bible, then, is the word of God. Every word of God is true (Prov. 30:5). We should expect it to be true, because the word of God reflects and expresses God, who is truth.

The people who have doubts about the truth of the Bible usually also have doubts about the truth of Jesus's teaching, because he taught that the Old Testament had divine authority. The modern cultural atmosphere is hostile to the idea that God could speak actual verbal discourses to finite human beings. But we must recognize this hostility for what it is. It is hostility in principle. The hostility is there among many people in the West even if they have not read a single verse of the Bible. They are already influenced by a cultural mood that rejects the idea of a divine voice. So it is not really the Bible that is their problem; it is the *God* of the Bible.[3] He is a God who speaks. And they have to quarrel with Jesus, because he accepted that God spoke in the Old Testament.

An Application

The presence of revelation is an encouragement and a motivation for us to respond with attentiveness, with care, and with obedience to what God shows us. Such response is appropriate both for general revelation and for special revelation. But when we are honest about our own situation and our own hearts, we have to admit that we are not worthy recipients. We fail to give thanks to God. We distort what we receive for selfish benefit. These failures are evidence of our need for redemption. So, as we proceed to later chapters, we take up the topics of our fallen, sinful state; the need for redemption; and how God has actually worked out redemption.

---

3 Cf. Poythress, *Inerrancy and Worldview.*

THE DOCTRINE OF MAN

8

The Origin and Nature of Mankind

MANKIND ORIGINATED according to the plan of God. The plan of God is one aspect of the truth of God. So the creation of mankind is in accord with the truth in God.

God Speaking

God speaks in order to execute his plan. Truth spoken is naturally in conformity with truth already existing, truth in the mind of God. This conformity between plan and speech holds true with respect to everything that God made. So it holds true when God creates mankind.

We cannot tell just from general principles what *details* are involved in how God made mankind. God has creative wisdom. He can create in more than one way. So we have to look at the details in the Bible if we want to know more.

Mankind in Communion with God

Mankind is like all other creatures in being specified and generated by the power of the word of God, which expresses the truth of God. We can see that God has designed us to receive and appreciate truth—truth that comes from him. So we must be creatures who are capable of receiving the truth and conforming to the truth. The truth originates in God. So the reception of the truth involves communion with God. That is, it involves communion with the Father, with the Son, and with the Holy Spirit. We are *personal* creatures, matching on the creaturely level the personal nature of God.

We can see, then, that we must mirror on the creaturely level the archetypal communication of truth in the Trinity. It is only a short step to say that we are in some sense an image of God. For example, we reflect him in the way in which the truth is among us. We can also see that we can speak and communicate to each other, on the creaturely level. When we do, we are imitating the archetypal speaking in the Trinity.

God's truth is associated with power to make things and events conform to the truth. Derivatively, in imitation of God, we have power to speak the truth, and some power, though limited, to shape the world. The Bible in Genesis 1:26, 28 becomes more specific. God gives us *dominion*. As one aspect of dominion, Adam is supposed to "work it [the garden] and keep it" (2:15). Later, Adam undertakes to name the animals:

> Now out of the ground the LORD God had formed every beast of the field and every bird of the heavens and brought them to the man to see what he would *call them*. And whatever the man *called* every living creature, that was *its name*. The man *gave names* to all livestock and to the birds of the heavens and to every beast of the field. But for Adam there was not found a helper fit for him. (2:19–20)

When Adam names the animals, it is a form of exercising authority over the animals. He is imitating the fact that God gave names in

Genesis 1 (vv. 5, 8, 10). Our ability to know truth and to speak naturally goes together with our unique role of dominion, in contrast to animals. Yes, animals have warning cries and noises for signaling. Ants pass chemical signals to one another, and honey bees communicate with dances. But there is no parallel among these animals with the complexity and depth of human communication. Human ability in this respect imitates divine ability.

We saw in chapter 1 that truth makes an absolute moral claim to our *allegiance*. Truth—and the God of truth—has a *moral* dimension. It is no surprise, then, that Adam and Eve come on the scene as morally responsible human beings. God expects obedience. That obedience includes the general principle that we should reflect God's holiness and purity. God also gives Adam a specific command with respect to the tree of the knowledge of good and evil (2:17).

We may add that morality exists in close connection with religion. Mankind is designed by God to have communion with God, as the presence of the tree of life hints (2:9). This tree symbolized that Adam and Eve were supposed to enjoy life in the presence of God. Life in the presence of God includes communion in the truth.

Mankind as the Image of God

In Genesis 1:26–27 the Bible becomes more specific about mankind. God indicates that he is going to make man "in our image, after our likeness" (compare 5:3). There is much discussion as to the meaning of "image" and "likeness" and what the implications are. It would deflect from our main purposes to enter into this discussion at length.

We may, however, venture to make a few observations on the basis of what we have already observed about the truth of God. We saw earlier that the Bible uses three main analogies for explaining relations among the persons of the Trinity: the analogy with communication, the analogy with a family, and the analogy with reflections. The first of these, the analogy with communication, has the closest and most obvious ties with the theme of the truth. But the second and the third also have a connection. Father and Son share a family love. As an aspect of this love, they share in the truth of God, with the Holy Spirit. And reflections share in the truth that they reflect. Let us call the original truth the *archetype*. It is reflected in a manifestation, which is derivative. We may call this reflection an *ectype*. Archetypal truth is reflected in ectypal truth.

This theme of reflections is closely related to the language about the image of God. If, as seems natural, we see the terms "image" and "likeness" as overlapping in their meanings in the key verses, both affirm that human beings in some respects reflect God. In fact, they reflect him in a host of ways. All the aspects of reflection involve analogy rather than identity. We are creatures, not the Creator. Yet we are like the Creator in being personal, in being able to know truth, in communicating, exercising dominion, and so on.

Man is the image of God. But he is an ectypal image. The archetypal image is the divine Son, who is "the image of the invisible God" (Col. 1:15) and "the exact imprint of his nature" (Heb. 1:3). This language of imaging is one prime way in which we affirm that man reflects God. The reality of reflection is in harmony with the fact that a truth that is expressed reflects the truth that it expresses. The truth that we know reflects the truth that God is and that he knows.

Adam and Modern Scientific Claims

Because of modern scientific claims, people have questions about how Genesis 1–3 relates to the idea of a gradual evolution. We must leave the details to other books.[1] But the main response is the same as with the doctrine of creation. Truth is unified. And God can act exceptionally, in miracles. The creation of Adam and Eve was his special work, not a gradual process over thousands of generations. If there is no God, or if God is uninvolved, there would be no plausible alternative to postulating some kind of gradual process; and that is one reason why we hear about a gradual process.

An Application

The dignity of the human race is an implication of the fact that we are made in the image of God and are capable of communion with God. We have a greatness, as creatures, that is not a matter of physical size but of personal significance. The story of the creation of mankind encourages us to admire whatever gifts other human beings have, and even our own gifts. Ultimately, the gifts come from God. They are not ours, as if we created them. So there is a ground for thanksgiving and for admiration, but not for a pride that displaces the glory that belongs to God.

Together with this dignity goes our shame. We have defaced the image of God in rebellion. There is much reason, then, both to thank God for who we are and to lament who we have become. The lament implies the need for salvation, a theme that still needs to be discussed.

1 Ann Gauger, Douglas Axe, and Casey Luskin, *Science and Human Origins* (Seattle: Discovery Institute Press, 2012); J. P. Versteeg, *Adam in the New Testament: Mere Teaching Model or First Historical Man?*, trans. Richard B. Gaffin Jr. (Phillipsburg, NJ: P&R, 2012).

9

The Original Covenant

FROM THE START, God has purposes as an aspect of his plan. He has purposes in the creation of human beings. Central to those purposes is the purpose of man having personal communion with God.

Two Trees

According to Genesis 2:9, in the garden of Eden there are two special trees. The tree of life and the tree of the knowledge of good and evil both function as symbols of aspects of communion with God. There is to be communion in life. God gives mankind life, and mankind enjoys communion with the archetypal life that is in God.

Life is closely connected to truth. When Jesus speaks to the Samaritan woman at the well, he offers her eternal life (John 4:14). Eternal life would come to her if she would ask (v. 10). At the same time, Jesus is explaining these things about life by his words. Life comes, not by magic, but by communion with Jesus. And this communion is expounded in words. The words come from Jesus, who is the Truth (14:6). It makes sense, then, that Jesus puts together the themes of the way, the truth, and the life in one verse referring to himself (14:6):

"I am the way, and the truth, and the life. No one comes to the Father except through me." In this verse, the way is the way to the truth that is in God; it is also the way to life—eternal life.

The tree of the knowledge of good and evil is also closely related to truth and to life with God. Its direct function is opposite to the tree of life. It is a tree that brings death if Adam or Eve choose to eat from it. Beyond this truth, interpreters dispute some aspects of its significance. It would appear that God has put it in the garden, and has spoken the specific prohibition, as a test. Through the test, Adam and Eve will come to a knowledge of good and evil.

They are supposed to come to a greater moral maturity in understanding good and evil according to God's moral standards. But the outcome can take place in either of two ways. If they succumb to the devil's temptation, they *do* come to know good and evil: "Behold, the man has become like one of us in *knowing good and evil*" (Gen. 3:22). This key verse is doubtless partly ironic, because Adam and Eve aspire to become godlike and yet the result is that they fall below their original standing. But it is only partly ironic. They do grow in experiential knowledge in the moral sphere. But they grow in the wrong way, in the way of disobedience. They *learn* (come to know) good and evil by experiencing it in disobedience. If, on the other hand, they had resisted the devil, they would have grown through obedience. They would have *experienced* and *learned* from experience what it means to obey and to resist temptation. They would have learned good by doing good; they would have learned evil by identifying it as a temptation and learning to resist it.

All these aspects are a matter of truth. The tree is specifically the tree of the *knowledge* of good and evil. Man has communion with God in the truth. As man experienced temptation, the temptation should have been an occasion for him to rely on God, to rely on God's word, to draw close to God, and to grow in his confidence in the truth and goodness of God's word. Communion should have taken place and grown right within the process of temptation. But in fact Adam failed. Communion with God was broken in the fall. Communion with the truth was broken. Adam failed to believe the truth about God's truthfulness and his goodness.

Where Is There a Covenant?

Interpreters differ in how they want to describe the situation before the fall, and whether it is to be understood as involving a covenant between God and man. The usual Hebrew word for *covenant* does not appear in Genesis 2–3. But it is not essential that it should. What we are asking about is rather the idea of communion between God and man. And we are asking whether that communion has moral dimensions. Do God's actions in relating to Adam and Eve have a moral dimension? And is the same true also of Adam and Eve as they act in relating to God?

Surely it is so. Truth has a moral dimension. It is morally absolute. If Adam and Eve are recipients of truth, they have obligations. They are recipients of a gift. This principle holds true as soon as Adam is created. And then it is true for Eve as soon as she is created. They are aware of truths about the world.

But the moral dimensions can be made explicit. And they do become more explicit when God speaks. He communicates truth in words. The truth that he communicates has its own moral dimensions. So we can actually plot four stages of moral responsibility:

1. Moral responsibility as soon as Adam is created, by virtue of the fact that he begins to receive truths about the world through general revelation.

81

2. Moral responsibility to receive with respect and obedience whatever God says to him.
3. Moral responsibility to act in a manner in conformity with God's plan for multiplication and dominion, expressed in Genesis 1:26, 28.
4. Moral responsibility to act in a manner in conformity with the specific instruction about the tree of the knowledge of good and evil, the instruction in 2:17.

These four stages are all expressions of truths about the personal and responsible relation between God and man. The stages are not isolated from each other, because, for one thing, they belong together in the comprehensive plan of God. When God first created Adam, in 2:7, he already had in mind the purposes that he specifically articulates in 1:26, 28 and 2:17. Those purposes are not an afterthought. Moreover, as we observed earlier, there is a long-range goal, namely the display of the glory of God in the new heaven and the new earth. That goal is implicit in God's rest on the seventh day.

Some people may want to be cautious, and say that a "covenant" is present only when the Bible uses the word *covenant* (or the equivalent in Hebrew, בְּרִית). According to that criterion, a "covenant" is not yet present in Genesis 1–2, because the specific word is not there. Other people may want to say that there is a covenant only when there are present explicitly all the features that come to be associated with later covenants, such as the feature of an official ratification ceremony. In that case, we do not have enough information to call the original relation between God and man a covenant. But there are still some features that are analogous to later explicit covenants. For example, like the later covenants, this early relation between God and humanity involves personal commitments and responsibility. Like later covenants, the word of God has what are called "stipulations," specifications of what is expected. God specifies, "You shall not eat . . ." (2:17). It is therefore in one sense a matter of taste as to whether we wish to use the word *covenant* more broadly or more narrowly, within the context of a technical discussion. I use the word *covenant* concerning these early stages in order to underline the analogies with the later stages.

These analogies are also linked with the theme of truth. Within the situation in Genesis 2, God communicates truth to Adam. The truth has a moral and religious obligation intrinsic to it. So the truths expressed in later covenants cohere with the truths expressed in the prefall situation with Adam.

Reward and Punishments

Genesis 2:17 becomes explicit about a punishment: "you shall surely die." The label for the tree of life suggests that it also articulates a consequence. It symbolizes the promise of life. With the two trees together, we have symbols of life and death, positive and negative. Actually, both trees have to do with both life and death. The tree of life obviously emphasizes the positive side, life. But to be barred from this tree would symbolize death. And that is what actually happens in Genesis 3:22–24. The tree of the knowledge of good and evil is directly linked to the threat of death. When God in 2:17 gives his warning about not eating from it, he says that eating from it results in death. So the emphasis is on the negative side, namely death. But the indirect implication is that if Adam and Eve do not eat from it, they will continue living. In fact, their obedience would enhance their life in fellowship with God.

We may also say that we have symbols of reward and punishment. Mankind can never "deserve" reward as if he were an equal with God. But God sets forth both reward and punishment in a manner fitting his character. The connection between obedience and life fits God's character and reflects it. God is life. He has eternal life. To live in obedience to him is to live in communion with the truth. Truth includes the commandment to which obedience responds (Deut. 5:33; 6:2; 32:46–47).

Righteousness and truth go together. The truth as an archetype is reflected in the truth that goes forth in expression. Righteousness has a symmetry too: "as you have done, it shall be done to you" (Obad. 15). If you live according to the truth and life that is in God, it shall be done to you according to truth and life—you shall have life and truth in abundance. This consequence is in accord with the bounty and beneficence of God, who delights to do good. It is also in accord with his righteousness. Since it is in accord with his righteousness, it is in accord with the truth about God, that he would reward obedience. Both the Old Testament and the New Testament indicate that God is pleased to reward obedience and punish disobedience: Genesis 4:7, 11–12; 6:13, 18, 22; Matt. 6:1, 20; etc.

Disobedience leads to death. What is human disobedience? Disobedience would destroy God, if it could, because any disobedience by implication sets up the self as the ultimate god. It says, implicitly, "I will be a god." It thinks in accord with what the serpent says: "you will be like God, knowing good and evil" (Gen. 3:5). And if someone thinks that he is a god, he tries to make God *not* to be God. He aims at destroying God's being God. The consequence is in accord with the principle of justice: "As you have done, it shall be done to you" (Obad. 15). God reflects his righteousness in a fitting punishment: the rebellious person gets destroyed by God, because he acted to destroy God. Death—the opposite of life in communion with God—is the form that destruction takes. Hell is the final and climactic expression of death (Rev. 20:14).

We have explicit teaching in Genesis 2:9 and 17 about deeds and their consequences. We can see that this explicit teaching harmonizes with the character of God, who is truth and justice and life. The working out of history, in the pattern of proposal (the commandment), test (obedience or disobedience), and reward follows from the nature of God's character.

Acknowledging Partial Knowledge

It is important to add that Genesis 2–3 does not fill in all the details that we might like to know. There is much that remains mysterious. This passage invites us to interpret it sensitively. We acknowledge that it is a comparatively sparse account. We acknowledge that God intends it to be supplemented by later revelations. These revelations do not add more details about the facts of what happened, but they do confirm that there is a general pattern of covenantal command, obligation, obedience, and disobedience. And we may say also that obedience springs from the heart. Merely outward obedience, hiding a grumbling heart, is not acceptable. The fundamental issue at the level of the heart is whether we love God or not (Deut. 6:5). Do we trust, then, that what he says is true and is for our good? Or do we listen to the serpent, who insinuates that God is withholding something that would be good for us?

The test for Adam is whether he will listen to truth, the truth of God, or to falsehood, the falsehood of the devil. The truth leads to life. The way of falsehood leads to death.

Both sides, life and death, are articulated in a context that has analogies with later covenants. In the later covenants, God speaks to specify the truth, which is truth about the relation of man to God and also about the obligations of man to God. The speech is binding speech, speech that has consequences.

The Framework of Covenant

This covenantal connection between God and man sets up a framework in which to understand the redeeming work of Christ. Christ came as the last Adam (1 Cor. 15:44–49), to keep covenant with God, to fulfill all righteousness (Matt. 3:15), and to offer us entrance into the covenant of grace, the covenant promising salvation through faith in Christ. But those topics are for later in this book.

An Application

The events in Genesis 3 confront us also, even today, with the question of life and death, as it applies to us. So the danger of sin must be taken to heart. Only redemption will deliver us from the jaws of death, jaws that we have already entered because of sinful hearts and sinful deeds.

10

The Fall

ADAM AND EVE did what God explicitly told them not to do: they ate of the special fruit. They sinned. They rebelled. They made themselves gods.

Corruption of the Truth

How could they have done what they did? They had everything. What caused them to doubt the faithfulness, truthfulness, and love of God? Yes, the serpent tempted them. But ultimately it is inexplicable why they yielded to the temptation. They were created good (Gen. 1:31). Unlike us, they did not have an inward inclination to evil that might rise up to meet the outward temptation.

Even when they sinned, however, they did not cease living in God's world. They did not cease being in the world. The world continued to be specified by truth, the truth of God. Sin does not escape the truth in every sense. Sin is a perversion of the truth, or a distortion of the truth. The distortion still has to be plausible. It still has to have fragments of truth, in order to be attractive. In the book of Revelation, Satan *counterfeits* the nature of God and the truth of God.

Corresponding to the three persons of the Trinity, there are in Revelation three counterfeit evil persons—Satan himself, the beast, and the false prophet (Rev. 16:13).[1]

We can see that distortion and counterfeiting in what the serpent says in Genesis 3:1, 4–5. Genesis 3:1 picks up on something that God actually did say. But it is distorted: "Did God actually say, 'You shall not eat of any tree of the garden'?" No, God did not say that. He said not to eat of *the one* tree, as Eve indicates. The serpent advances the first phase of his deceit by initially putting the issue in the form of a question. At least at first, he does not directly contradict what God says. He simply makes an inquiry. But questions are not always innocent. A question can insinuate something. And this one does. It insinuates that God is not generous.

At the next stage, the serpent directly contradicts what God said. In verse 4 he says, "You will not surely die." Then he goes on to depict what will happen if Eve eats. And what he says actually turns out to be true. Their eyes were opened (v. 7). And they came to know good and evil (v. 22). But both of these results of their action contain distortions. Their eyes were opened to their nakedness and to their guilt. The serpent made his tempting words sound like something good, an advance in understanding. But the fruit turned out to be bitter.

In addition, as indicated earlier, the man and the woman became "like God" in knowing good and evil, but in the wrong way, in the experience of evil in themselves.

In these ways, the entrance of evil does not completely destroy truth. Rather, it distorts truth. But in this way it is still dependent on truth.

---

1   Vern S. Poythress, *The Returning King: A Guide to the Book of Revelation* (Phillipsburg, NJ: P&R, 2000), 138–48.

Propagation of Evil

Truth propagates. It propagates eternally from the Father to the Son, who is the Word. It propagates to earth when the plan of God leads to the created world. It propagates to mankind, in their being in the image of God. It propagates to them when God speaks to them. This propagation ought to continue. We may infer that Adam informed Eve of the commandment not to eat of the tree of the knowledge of good and evil. From the beginning, it can be inferred that Adam and Eve ought to instruct their children in the truth that they have received from God (Deut. 6:6–9). In this instruction, they would be imitating God, who instructed them. They would be *reflecting* God by reflecting the truth and communicating it.

To some extent, even after the fall, such propagation continues. The key promise of redemption in Genesis 3:15 is preserved in the record of Genesis. It is operative also in the line of promise, which Genesis traces from Adam to Seth (rejecting Cain), to Noah, to Shem (not Ham and Japheth), to Abraham, and to Abraham's descendants.

Sin, as a distortion of the truth, also has its propagation. Ironically, mankind after the fall still reflects God—he images God—but in a reversed way, by propagating sin. We see sin grow in its proportions in the line of Cain. It grows until the earth is filled with wickedness (Gen. 6:5). We might also infer that the earth is filled with lies. The fundamental lie is that God is not God, and that we can get away with wickedness. Even that is a distortion of the truth. Cain suffered punishment for his murder, but he did not die for it. To that extent, he "got away" with it. Lamech seems to have "gotten away" with his boasting and his threats (Gen. 4:24). People got away with multiplying wickedness, up to the point of Genesis 6:5, just before the flood. From a human point of view, justice is not always executed speedily (Eccles. 8:11).

Death, as the penalty for sin, also propagates. With the exception of Enoch, the genealogy of Genesis 5 has the grim repeated expression "and he died."

The indirect consequences of sin also multiply. The woman has pain in childbearing. The man has pain in working the ground (Gen. 3:16–19).

Federal Representation

Does Adam's sin propagate itself to his descendants in sinful human nature? Does the guilt of Adam propagate? Are we guilty not only for our own individual sins and for our own individual sinful nature, but for Adam's guilt?

Genesis 2–3 does not *directly* tell us. It is a narrative reporting the events that happened. Like most narratives, it is sparse. It leaves out a lot. For the most part, it *shows* what happened, rather than developing a theological treatise explaining the meaning of the fall.[2] Genesis 3 is followed by Genesis 4–6. These chapters show us, rather than telling us, that sin grows and propagates. It remains for later expository material, such as Romans 5:12–21 and 1 Corinthians 15:21–26, to become more explicit and more reflective about the theological meaning of Adam and his relation to his descendants. It is rightly the case that theological reflections on Adam and on the covenant with Adam mainly use

2 V. Philips Long, *The Reign and Rejection of King Saul: A Case for Literary and Theological Coherence* (Atlanta: Scholars Press, 1989), 31–34; Vern S. Poythress, *Interpreting Eden: A Guide to Faithfully Reading and Understanding Genesis 1–3* (Wheaton, IL: Crossway, 2019), 128–30.

these later passages as the primary sources for setting forth the idea of Adam as federal head—as representative—of the human race.

The idea of representation is itself fairly common in the Bible. Tribal heads represent their tribes. David represents the whole Israelite army when he fights Goliath. David's victory is a victory for all of Israel (1 Sam. 17:9, 52–53). The king represents the people. Likewise, the high priest represents the people. The modern West has been influenced by a radical individualism which discounts or scoffs at corporate solidarity. But modern bias should not be allowed to blind us to the presence of these instances of representation. In the case of the high priest, God himself established the high priest's representative role. Likewise, God appointed Adam as a representative for the human race.

We can also see a kind of analogy to human representation in the nature of truth. Truth itself is one united whole in the mind of God. Any one truth is the truth of God and is joined in solidarity with all the other truths in God's mind. Each truth is in harmony with all other truths. Each exists in the environment of the other truths. Each calls to mind other, related truths. So we can say that a single truth stands for truth in general. We might say that one truth *represents* many truths. In particular, one truth represents many instances of that truth. If this connectedness exists in the realm of truth, it may also exist in the realm of human endeavors. It should not be surprising, then, that there are larger unities, beyond the level of individual human beings. Each individual is responsible as an individual (Ezek. 18:20; Rev. 20:13). But he is not isolated.

We must also be ready to recognize that Adam, as the head of the entire human race, is unique. As Romans 5:12–21 and 1 Corinthians 15:21–26 remind us, Christ is also unique. In a manner similar to Adam being the head of the old humanity, Christ is the head of the new humanity. As Adam's sin made the race guilty, so Christ's righteousness makes his new humanity righteous (Rom. 5:16–19).

An Application

Let us learn to reckon with the propagation of sin. Let us flee from its path by fleeing to Christ, our redeemer.

11

Free Agency

EARLIER WE ARGUED that the origin of truth in God implies that God is comprehensively ruling the world. His rule encompasses also the decisions and actions of every human being. But if this is so, is it compatible with human responsibility and with our intuition that we make free choices?

Dual Causation

A partial relief can be found in the idea of dual causation. God brings about events as the "primary cause" of the events. Human beings act as "secondary causes."

This distinction may seem artificial. But it is compatible with the nature of truth—truth originating in God. Truth in God is comprehensive. It specifies everything. And that specification includes all forms of causation. Not only things but events are specified. And not only events but causal connections between events. So when one billiard ball hits another, and the second ball begins to move, the causal connection between the two balls is real.

The original or archetypal cause is to be found in God. God speaks his Word. He sends out the Word as his speech. We may say that the

Father "causes" the Word. But we must, as usual, be careful how we understand the relation between the Father and the Word. It is an eternal relation, as John 1:1 affirms by saying "in the beginning." The Word always exists, rather than having a moment of coming into existence. Verse 3 confirms the eternal existence of the Word by indicating that "all things were made through him." The Word himself, the eternal Son, was not made. He was not created, but exists forever. At the same time, there is something like an eternal "motion" from the Father to the Word. We have reformulated this relation in terms of the truth. The Word is the expression of the truth of God.

Further expressions of the truth take place when God creates the world. For example, God said, "Let there be light," and there was light (Gen. 1:3). It is true that God is light (1 John 1:5). It is also true that light (as a created phenomenon) exists in the world. Created light reflects God, who is light. The truth about created light reflects the truth about God being light. In addition, we know as we read further on in Genesis 1 that, in a special way, human beings are a kind of "reflection" of God. Man is made in the *image* of God (Gen. 1:26–27). He reflects God. As one aspect of this reflection, the truths that he comes to know reflect the truths that God knows.

Causes as Reflection

If truth reflects itself in the world, there can also be a kind of reflection of causation. The archetype for causation is found in the eternal begetting of the Son. (But as the divine archetype, it is different from causation within the created world.) This archetype, in eternal begetting, may reflect itself in the world. So then, there can be causes *in* the world. The events of the crucifixion are a crucial case. God brought about the events. But it is also the case that there were human agents who acted according to their own desires: "this Jesus, delivered up according to the definite plan and foreknowledge of God, you crucified and killed by the hands of lawless men" (Acts 2:23; compare Acts 4:25–28).

Since mankind is uniquely in the image of God, we may find it natural that causation *in* the world has more than one layer of reflection. Human causation through human intention is one layer of cause. But when my arm throws a ball, my arm and the muscles in it act as a *physical* layer of cause.

This multilayering of causes is confirmed by the account in Job 1–2.

First, God causes the disasters that fall on Job, as Job himself asserts in 1:21 and 2:10. Some modern people find themselves wanting to shrink from this conclusion. They want to "protect" God by denying that he brought about calamities. But this route will not work. The testimony of the Bible is against it. The Bible shows that Job affirms God's control over calamities: "The LORD gave, and the LORD has taken away" (Job. 1:21). And it approves Job's affirmations: "In all this Job did not sin with his lips" (2:10).

Second, Satan brings the disasters. Job and his friends never learn about this level of causation, but the book of Job affirms it in its first two chapters: "So Satan went out from the presence of the LORD and struck Job with loathsome sores from the sole of his foot to the crown of his head" (2:7).

Third, for some of the disasters there are human agents. "The oxen were plowing and the donkeys feeding beside them, and the Sabeans fell upon them and took them and struck down the servants with the edge of the sword, and I alone have escaped to tell you" (Job 1:14–15).

Fourth, some of the disasters involve physical causes, such as fire (v. 16) and "a great wind" (v. 19).

Understanding Human Agency as a Reflection

We may better appreciate human agency if we approach it "from above," starting with God's agency. God is personal. And God acts in the world. In his actions, he makes *choices*. He is a responsible, personal agent, not just a mindless, physical cause like fire or wind. He *chose* to send the fire and the wind and the other disasters that befell Job. In the light of God's personal agency, what do we learn about human agents? Human agents are not God, but they reflect God's agency on a lower level.

We may also express this mystery of agency in terms of our theme of truth. It is true that God makes *choices*. For example, it is true that God sent the "fire of God" that "fell from heaven" in Job 1:16 and "burned up the sheep and the servants." That truth is bound up with a decision by God to act in one way and not another. Other truths are truths that express a necessity in God's character. For instance, God is necessarily good. The freedom of choice that God has in sending fire is also a kind of freedom about what truths are true. If God had wished, he could have refrained from sending fire, and it would have been the truth that no fire came.

By analogy, human beings exercise a freedom of choice when they decide to do one thing rather than another. Starting with God and his freedom, we move by analogy to human beings and their freedom.

Difficulties with Trying to Understand "from Below"

Let us contrast this process of reasoning from God to mankind with a movement "from below." We can get into difficulty if we try to understand human action "from below," merely by comparison with physical causation. Is human action like one billiard ball bouncing off another (physical causation)? In some ways it is, because both actions are "causes" of some sort. The first billiard ball *causes* the second one to move. A human being causes the cue stick in his hand to move and hit the billiard ball, by deciding to move the stick. But if there were only one level of cause, namely physical cause, where would be the sense of human responsibility and the genuineness of human choice? The billiard ball is not responsible and does not have a choice. It does whatever the first ball causes it to do. The human being who controls a cue stick *does* have freedom of choice ("free agency").

Suppose for the sake of argument that there is only one level of causation, namely physical causation. Then human action, like all other instances of action, takes place by an unbroken link of physical causes, and that alone. If the chain is unbroken, it appears that free agency and human responsibility are illusory. There is no real choice. All results are determined by earlier physical causes. Some of the physical causes are outside a human being's body (like the billiard ball that hits another ball). Other physical causes are inside a human body (like the signals from nerves and the chemical reactions leading to the contraction of muscles in a person's arms and fingers). But all these are physical causes.

When we see this difficulty, we may try to escape by postulating a *break* in the links of physical causation. We postulate that, at some point, there is something new, something uncaused. We may then try claiming that the break represents an instance of "free will." But if the break is completely uncaused and unmotivated, it has no responsibility attached to it. It is mere randomness, mere chance. So again, there is nothing we can easily recognize as *human* choice, where *we* have intentions that we bring to fruition. Nor is there human responsibility, but only something unaccountable and uncontrolled.

So how can we understand human responsibility? It is something that does *not* belong to rocks and billiard balls. What makes human beings different? We are made in the image of God. God has made us with the ability to take initiative and to make responsible decisions. It appears, then, that human freedom is derivative from divine freedom, which is its archetype. This is mysterious.

Two Attributes of God

We do not know God comprehensively. He is mysterious to us. But we can trace out some of the meaning of two aspects in God: his stability (unchangeability) and his freedom (creativity). Both have to be true. God is who he is, and he cannot be anything other than who he is. But God is also creative. His creativity is displayed in the fact that he created the world. He did not have to create (that would in the end make him dependent on the world). He was also independent and creative when he sent fire from heaven on Job's sheep (Job 1:16). Nothing above him or behind him forced him to do it. (If there were something behind him that controlled him, that other thing would be the real "god.")

Now let us focus on God's stability, his faithfulness. His stability, or his unchangeability, belongs to each person of the Trinity—to the Father, to the Son, and to the Holy Spirit. In addition, as we have seen earlier, the stability of God is preeminently expressed in God the Father, who is the source of God's unchanging plan.

In addition, God is *creative*. His creativity is preeminently exemplified in God the Son, who is the Word. God speaks, expressing his intentions. And instances of that speech include speaking to the world: "Let there be light." God did not *need* to say that. He made a choice to say it.

Two Aspects of Truth

We may reformulate this principle in terms of the theme of truth. All truth is a unified whole in the mind of God. But we can also note that the truths about God are of two distinct kinds. There are truths about him that are true because of who he always is. He is infinite, unchangeable, and omniscient. There are also truths that express his creative wisdom. He *decided* to create a world, rather than just to be God forever with no act of creation. He *decided* to send fire from heaven on Job's sheep. We must have a distinction of this kind, because God himself is necessary but the world is not necessary. There is therefore a distinction between truths about the world and truths that describe God's eternal existence.

We may say, therefore, that truth has two aspects. There are *necessary* truths, truths about who God always is. And there are *contingent* truths, truths about the world that God decided to create and truths about acts that he accomplishes in the world. These latter truths are *contingent* in the sense that they depend on God's free decision to create the world. God presumably *could* have created a different world than the world we actually have. That too illustrates his freedom and creativity. He could have created a world with unicorns, but he did not. He could have sent fire from heaven in such a time and a place that no harm would come to Job's sheep. He could have planted the maple trees in our back yard in a different location. God is *free* and *creative.*

The presence of both kinds of truth—necessary truths and contingent truths—is a mystery. We cannot analyze it to the bottom. But we can accept that truth is in harmony with God.

This presence of freedom in God is then reflected in mankind. We have a kind of derivative freedom, a freedom that reflects God's freedom.

We may re-express these truths by discussing the freedom we exercise when we speak. God speaks. Human beings, as creatures derivative from God, say things. They are responsible for what they say. (We may allow exceptions due to special circumstances, such as in dreams and in comas and in cases of dementia.) Humans make choices. We can see that there are alternatives that could have been said, but that they chose not to say.

This responsibility and choice-making is derivative from God. It is mysterious. We are not God. We are not acting independent of God, because "In him we live and move and have our being" (Acts 17:28). Rather, there are two levels of causation. God brings about all events whatsoever, including human speech (Lam. 3:37–38; Eph. 1:11). Simultaneously, we speak. Each of us causes his own speech, through his intentions. And of course there is a physical level of causation, through lungs and diaphragm and vocal chords and mouth and tongue and lips. This level of physical causation is real. But because it is a *distinct* level, it does not undermine the reality that *we* as human beings act with personal intention. For example, I move a cue stick and set a billiard ball in motion, so that it hits another billiard ball. *I* am setting the cue stick in motion, by choosing my angle and force. At the same time, physical causes in my muscles are resulting in the cue stick being in motion.

This multilevel causation, as we have seen, is not surprising, because it is in conformity with the multilayer reflection of truth in the world.

Depravity

In connection with the fall of mankind and the issue of free agency, we have to look at the issue of depravity. Are people so twisted and perverted by the fall and by sin that they cannot by their own power climb their way out of sin and into redemption? Most Christians reading the Bible have understood over the centuries that God says that human beings need divine assistance (Luke 18:27). But what form does this assistance take? And does God assist everyone equally?

As with other issues that we discuss in this book, we cannot take the space to consider all the ins and outs of all arguments, using every text of the Bible that is pertinent (there are many such texts). We are rather looking to see how the perspective of truth harmonizes with and confirms what we have come to know from the Bible.

One of the core issues is this: who makes the really decisive contribution, God or man? If God does, one possible conclusion is that salvation is fatalistic and that human beings have lost their responsibility. If man makes the decisive contribution, then he has something to boast in, however small a contribution it may be.

Our meditations on the truth, and the origin of truth in God, lead to a framework in which it is natural to say that the decisive contribution is from God. First Corinthians 4:7 is relevant: "What do you have that you did not receive? If then you received it, why do you boast as if you did not receive it?" We are fundamentally recipients of gifts. We do nothing without the gift of power to do it. Any truths that we know, we know because we have received them from God. Likewise, any powers that we have to act come from God. Now, our reception of a gift from God involves active human processes and active intentionality. It involves human choice. For example, we are active in various ways when we receive truths from God. We digest truths that we receive. But the reception of the gift is a reception engendered by God. God brought redemption to us, and has worked it in us, through faith, which is the gift of God (Eph. 2:8).

Let us consider salvation from the perspective of truth. God sends forth his truth, in the message of the gospel. This truth proclaims the truth of the work of Christ, accomplished in history. And by the power of Christ's resurrection, truth begets new life in us:

> . . . since you have been born again, not of perishable seed but of imperishable, through the living and abiding *word of God*; for

"All flesh is like grass
and all its glory like the flower of grass.
The grass withers,
and the flower falls,
but the word of the Lord remains forever."

And this word is the good news that was preached to you. (1 Pet. 1:23–25)

It is customary to think of new birth as brought about by the Holy Spirit. And this role of the Holy Spirit is affirmed in John 3:5–8. That is not in tension with what is said in 1 Peter 1:23–25, since the Holy Spirit is present in the word of God, which is the truth of God.

As fallen, sinful human beings, we deserve death. We are guilty rebels. If God acts to save us, it is not because we deserve it. It is because God decides on his own initiative to be merciful to us.

An Application

If we are already saved, let us pray that God would preserve us and that he would bring others to salvation. Only God can do these things. If we are not already saved, let us come to Christ to save us, because only God can save us.

PART III

REDEMPTION

12

The Person of Christ

LET US NOW CONSIDER the person of Christ.

God the Son exists forever as one of the three persons of the Trinity. He is the Truth (John 14:6), even before he came to earth and became man. We have already addressed this aspect of the person of Christ.

But there are additional truths that need to be examined. They concern Christ as redeemer. For the sake of us and our salvation, the eternal Son became man (John 1:14; Heb. 2:14, 17). Since the moment of his incarnation, he is one person with two natures, namely his divine nature and his human nature. Christians over the ages have recognized that this existence in two natures is a great mystery.

Incarnation and Truth

It is true that Jesus Christ has two natures, divine and human. But this truth cannot be a matter of deduction from the nature of God. God did not have to create the world. Nor, after the fall of man, was he under any innate obligation to save the world. He undertook to save human beings out of his mercy. This was planned before the foundation of the world, according to 1 Pet. 1:20–21: "He [Christ] was

foreknown before the foundation of the world but was made manifest
in the last times for the sake of you who through him are believers in
God, . . ."His mercy is free, not obligated, according to the very nature
of mercy. The incarnation did not take place because of some innate
deficiency in mankind as a created being. Rather, it was one phase in
the working out of God's plan of *redemption.*

In accordance with our general purpose in this book, we will not
take time to review the full spectrum of biblical teaching that supports
our conclusions about Christ. Rather, we will consider the person
and work of Christ from the standpoint of truth as a perspective. In
particular, we may consider how the nature of Christ, as one person
with two natures, is in harmony with the truth.

Harmony with Truth

The incarnation is in harmony with the truth because it is true. But we
may move at least a little bit beyond this elementary observation by
recalling that the eternal Son is also "the image of the invisible God"
(Col. 1:15). And then, as a further truth, God created man in the
image of God (Gen. 1:26–27). The created image, the image in man,
is a reflection of the archetypal image, which is the Son. The truth
about the created image reflects the truth about the uncreated Image,
the archetypal image, who is the divine Son (Col. 1:15). So there is
intrinsic harmony between the Son, who is the archetypal image, and
a human being, who is an ectypal or derivative image.

This harmony is then the basis for the incarnation. It seems to us
paradoxical to affirm that Jesus Christ as God knows all things (John
16:30; Col. 2:3), while with respect to his human nature he is limited
in knowledge (Luke 2:52). How can his knowledge be comprehensive
and also be limited at the same time? We give what answer we can

give to this question when we distinguish the two natures. But there is only one person.

Distinguishing but Not Separating

We cannot form an exact model of what it means to "experience" knowledge in two natures. Each of us has only one nature, our human nature. Jesus Christ is unique. But we can affirm a harmony because, even in the case of our ordinary human nature, none of our knowledge exists except in communion with and in dependence on divine knowledge. We do not know how the two natures of Christ can exist together in one person, without confusion, without change, without division, and without separation, as the Chalcedonian Creed says.[1] But neither do we know in a transparent way how the Holy Spirit dwells in us and gives us truth.

The Spirit is the source of truth, as Job 32:8 hints:

But it is the spirit in man,

the breath of the Almighty, that makes him understand.

The Spirit is God. How can truth go from God to us? It must be without confusion, since we do not become divine. It must be without a change in God, because God does not change. Truth, when received by us, changes us in a sense. We know more than we did before. But it does not make us less human.

When the truth comes from God to us, the truth in us is not "divided" or "separated" from the truth in God, or it would be no truth at all. So in the process of truth coming to us we have an analogy to the affirmations in the Chalcedonian Creed that we noted above.

1 Cf. Philip Schaff, *The Creeds of Christendom: With a History and Critical Notes* (New York: Harper & Brothers, 1890), 2.62–65.

The Creator/Creature Distinction

We should not be completely surprised. To be a personal creature involves two sides simultaneously. We are creatures, and then also we are persons who have the capability of having communion with God. In redemption, we do have communion with God the Creator. There must be distinctions, of course, if the Creator/creature distinction is to remain valid. And we have seen already that it is valid, because it reflects the archetypal distinction between the Father and the Son, who is the mediator of creation, whose word structures the creation.

At the same time, there must be communion. What we know must be intimately tied to what God knows, because all truth is in him, as archetype.

A Necessity for Redemption

For any human being, redemption requires something more than that the human being know facts about God. There is guilt, liability, and demerit, which weigh us down and which have to be dealt with. We have to face the punishment of death, which, without redemption, will come in our future if God does not undertake to redeem us from the punishment. "The wages of sin is death" (Rom. 6:23). We need God to save us. We need a man to be united to us, to substitute for us, and to bring us out of our misery. Our Savior must be God, in order to have the power to save us. He must also become man, in order to substitute for us as our sin bearer. In addition, we need to be born again, to become a new creation in Christ (2 Cor. 5:17).

An Application

Let us thank God for his wisdom in planning and accomplishing redemption for us in Jesus Christ, God and man.

13

Christ as Prophet, King, and Priest

THE DAMAGE DONE by sin is many-sided. Correspondingly, the redemption brought about by Christ must be many-sided. Classically, one way in which his work has been expounded is in terms of three biblical offices, namely prophet, king, and priest.[1]

The Three Offices as Derivative from the Truth

The Bible indicates that Christ is the final prophet, king, and priest. The book of Hebrews teaches us about all three offices. Christ is the culmination of the Old Testament prophets, according to Hebrews 1:1–2. He is the final priest, according to Hebrews 7–10. His kingly rule is described in Hebrews 2:8–9.

Though these three offices belong to Christ as one person, we can see a way in which the distinction between offices traces back to the distinction of persons in the Trinity. Let us see how this works out.[2]

---

1 Philip Schaff, *The Creeds of Christendom: With a History and Critical Notes* (New York: Harper & Brothers, 1890), 3.307 (Heidelberg Catechism, Question 31). Also the Westminster Confession of Faith, 8.1; Westminster Shorter Catechism, QQ. 23–26; Westminster Larger Catechism, 42–45.

2 Vern S. Poythress, *Knowing and the Trinity: How Perspectives in Human Knowledge Imitate the Trinity* (Phillipsburg, NJ: P&R, 2018), ch. 15.

Let us recall that there are three main analogies for the Trinity, namely the analogy with communication, the analogy with a family, and the analogy with reflections. Any one of these analogies expresses to us the reality of the Trinity. But there are distinct emphases.

The analogy with communication focuses on the truth as communicated to us, especially the truth that comes in verbal articulations. It is a primary role of the prophet to bring the truth of God to the people whom God addresses. So the analogy with communication is closely tied to the office of prophet.

The analogy with a family is the analogy that is used when the Father is called Father and the Son is called Son. This analogy seems to be primary when we consider the working out of God's plan in time. God the Father is preeminently the planner. God the Son does the will of the Father and executes his plan, especially during the Son's public ministry on earth. God the Holy Spirit applies the redemption accomplished by the Son. All of this work is work in *power*. A human king who serves God works in power to execute the plan of God. Christ is the divine king who carries out the plan of God for redemption. Thus he is the final and climactic *king*. The truth has a role in this analogy and in the work of the king. Christ the king carries out the plan of the Father, and the plan is a plan that is the truth about history.

Finally, the analogy with reflections is an analogy that focuses on presence, on intimacy. In the working of redemption, intimacy with God, enjoyment of the presence of God, is worked out preeminently by the priests. Christ is the great and final priest, after the order of Melchizedek (Heb. 5:10). So the office of priest is closely related to the analogy with reflections.

This enjoyment of the presence of God is also enjoyment of the intimacy of knowing God and therefore also knowing the truth, because God is truth.

Because the fall and sin have brought disruption, Christ's work in all three offices has a negative as well as a positive side. With respect to his work as prophet, he overcomes and drives out error by proclaiming the truth.

With respect to his work as king, he overcomes Satan, the chief opponent. He uses his kingly power to subdue Satan. He also overcomes rebellion and disobedience to the king by subduing us and ruling over us. In his rule over us, he also conforms us to the true standard of his righteousness. By his power he makes the truth to be manifest and effective in the world.

With respect to his work as priest, he overcomes alienation and the penalty of death. He is not only the priest, but the sacrifice, who dies on our behalf. Positively, he presents us in purity to God the Father (Heb. 10:14) and intercedes for us (Heb. 7:25). He opens the way for us to have renewed communion with God, and therefore also communion with the truth that resides in God. We need communion in order to have access to the truth. Psalm 119:18 says, "Open my eyes, that I may behold wondrous things out of your law."

The need for access to the truth holds even for non-Christians, for unbelievers. They distort the truth about God, but they do not completely lose access to the truth. We can infer that the truths they receive in this life are gifts of common grace. They are not deserved. Common grace is not saving grace. That is to say, the fact that people receive some benefits from God does not imply that they are heirs of eternal salvation. But to receive what they do not deserve is nevertheless a benefit, a non-saving benefit that overflows from the work of

Christ. Unbelievers have fragments of the truth (see Ps. 94:10). And yet, their knowledge is defective, because they do not accept these truths in the context of knowing the God who is working salvation.

We can see a picture of this kind of benefit in the incident immediately after the flood of Noah in Genesis 8:20–22. Noah offers sacrifices to God (v. 20). These sacrifices prefigure the final sacrifice of Christ. The animal sacrifices are accepted by God by virtue of their prefiguring what Jesus will do (Heb. 10:1–10). God is pleased with the sacrifices and makes a promise of benefits to Noah and his descendants, not all of whom are believers in the true God.

In short, one of the consequences of Christ's work is that even unbelievers receive benefits of grace. One such benefit is the promise that God will not again destroy humanity as a whole with a flood. It is also a benefit that they receive pieces of truth.

An Application

Let us thank the Lord for giving us truth, power to change, and intimacy with God, through Christ, who is prophet, king, and priest.

14

Christ's Atoning Work

IT IS CHRIST who reconciles us to God. He is "the way" (John 14:6). How does his work of reconciliation take place?

One important aspect of his work of reconciliation is that he has borne our sins (1 Pet. 2:24; also Isa. 53:4–6; 2 Cor. 5:21). He became our substitute in taking the punishment that was due for our sins. But how do we understand such a substitutionary work? Christ's substitutionary work is unique. It is not comparable to anything else. Perhaps the closest comparison appears in Romans 5:12–21, in the parallels between Christ and Adam. But even here, the comparison underlines differences: "But the free gift *is not like* the trespass" (v. 15); "much more" (vv. 15, 17).

A General Pattern of Substitution

Granted the uniqueness of Christ's work, we can still note how there are broader patterns of substitution. For example, the high priest in Leviticus 16 represents the whole people of Israel (v. 21). The death of the Passover lamb and the death of other sacrificial animals substitute for the death that the people of Israel would otherwise receive. When

David fights Goliath in 1 Samuel 17, he represents the entire Israelite army, and in a certain respect substitutes for it.

Situations where one person substitutes for another involve both similarities and differences. The two people differ from each other, by being two. But when one substitutes for another, he steps into the same or a parallel role.

We may see that there are broader analogies for such similarities and differences if we first take a step back from the details. We consider the general structure of truth, as it exists in the mind of God.

A study of truth in relation to the persons of the Trinity shows a pattern of similarity and difference. The truth known by each person of the Trinity is the same truth. That offers us the dimension of similarity. In addition, each person knows the truth personally. For example, the Father knows the truth in knowing the Son; the Son knows the truth in knowing the Father (Matt. 11:27). The aspect of difference with respect to truth lies in the personal *view* or *perspective* on the truth. This difference includes a structure where one person images another in a formulation, and the result is still true. For example, we may start with saying that the Father knows the truth. We say also that the Son knows the truth. And likewise the Spirit knows the truth. There is commonality in the three. But the persons are distinct.

These affirmations do not undermine the permanent distinction between the Father and the Son, and between the Father and the Spirit. In fact, precisely because the Father and the Son are distinct, there are distinctions between distinct truths. It is true that the Father knows the Son; it is true that the Son knows the Father. And these two truths are distinct. But they are also *related.* They are related in terms of the way in which one person "images" another within one context.

We must also note differences in the truths about the distinct persons. For example, the Son, not the Father, took on human nature and became incarnate. This incarnation was unique to the Son. So the truths about the Son and about the Father are not parallel at this point.

When God undertakes to communicate truth to us, a structure of imaging is present. Consider John 17:8: "For I [the Son] have given them [the disciples] the words that you [the Father] gave me." We may see two stages:

The Father gives words to the Son.
The Son gives words to the disciples.

There are two instances of imaging or reflection in the second line. The Son images the Father, while the disciples image or reflect the Son. At the same time, it is the same words that are referred to in each of the two lines. And therefore also, it is the same complex of truths to which the two lines refer.

We can also observe a pattern of imaging within the created order:

When Adam had lived 130 years, he fathered a son in his own likeness, after his image, and named him Seth. (Gen. 5:3)

That is, Seth is the image of Adam.

All these instances are what we might call unproblematic instances of imaging or reflection. The case with Adam and Seth is particularly noteworthy. It was not merely an accident that Adam fathered a son. Adam was imitating—on a creaturely level—what happened when God made Adam in his image (Gen. 1:26–27). There is a genuine common pattern, a pattern of "fathering." And of course the pattern continues. Seth fathered a son named Enosh (5:6). Enosh fathered Kenan (5:9). And so on.

So we can see that a pattern of imaging or reflection is innate in the created order (Adam and Seth and Enosh and Kenan). Each son replicates the pattern of his father by becoming a father in turn. This kind of replication of a pattern is a general form of substitution. Moreover, the pattern finds its origin beyond the created order. The archetype, as usual, is God himself. The persons of the Trinity are equally God. So in many contexts (but not all) they may reflect or image one another in our formulations of truth. The Father is omnipotent; the Son is omnipotent; and the Holy Spirit is omnipotent.

Problematic Substitution to Overcome a Deficit

In the wake of the fall, there must be a substitution in another dimension in order to overcome sin and its consequences. We can see a symbolic picture of the propagation of sin in the provisions for uncleanness. Death is a symbol for sin, as well as the ultimate consequence of sin. The Israelites become unclean if they touch a dead body, whether it is the dead body of a human being or the body of an animal that has died of itself (Lev. 11:31–39). Uncleanness propagates. There is a kind of one-way replacement, in that we move from the truth that the dead body is unclean to the new state of things, namely that the person who has touched it is now unclean. In certain situations, holiness also propagates in a one-way fashion. In Leviticus 27, if a person endeavors to substitute a new animal for the one that is already devoted to God, both become devoted (Lev. 27:10, 33).

Death is the ultimate enemy. So Christ gives himself over to death in order to redeem those under death's power. His death comes on him because of them. He substitutes for them (Heb. 2:14–15). He represents them. He replaces them in undergoing judgment. He defeats the devil in death, in order that we might be released from death. We can see here also a second phase. Christ does not remain permanently dead but rises again. And so his followers rise spiritually to new life, free from the power of the devil.

One of the dimensions of the work of Christ is victory over the devil and releasing those who were captive to him (Matt. 12:29). There are two phases of this substitutionary work. Christ undergoes death, substituting for those whom he redeems. Second, Christ overcomes the devil. This overcoming by Christ affects those who are redeemed, so that they are released from Satan's captivity.

Christ's substitution for us makes sense because Christ is the representative for each of us who is redeemed, and for redeemed humanity as a whole. His work parallels the role of Adam (Rom. 5:12–21; 1 Cor. 15:44–49). As we have said, this substitution is unique, because Christ is unique. But it has an affinity with the theme of imaging and reflections. And the theme of reflections in turn has an affinity with the theme of truth. The truth in God the Father is expressed and reflected in the Son. And the truth of God is reflected on the level of creatures when human beings know the truth.

Penal Substitution

Another dimension of Christ's work concerns the penalty for sin. He bears the penalty of others, according to 1 Peter 2:24 and Isaiah 53:5. Those on behalf of whom he suffers are therefore released from penalty. But there is a second phase. Christ's resurrection is his vindication and his triumph over death. This vindication counts for those who belong to him: "It will be counted to us who believe in him who raised from the dead Jesus our Lord, who was delivered up for our trespasses and raised for our justification" (Rom. 4:24–25).

Modernist theology has an antipathy to penal substitution (that is, the reality that Christ substituted for us by taking the penalty for sin). It is considered irrational. But the real irrationalism is to try to be more rational than God! In fact, patterns of substitution are widespread, not only in the Bible, but even outside, in false religions and in flawed systems of justice. Modernism has in its arrogance discarded whatever it cannot fit into its own impoverished framework.

Christ is a substitute for us with respect to the wrath of God. This truth is uncomfortable for modernism, but it is an undeniable theme in the Bible. Christ became a curse to deliver us from the curse (Gal. 3:13): "Christ redeemed us from the curse of the law by becoming a curse for us." The next verse in Galatians 3, verse 14, deals with a second phase, inheriting blessing. Christ as the offspring has inherited the blessing: "so that in Christ Jesus the blessing of Abraham might come to the Gentiles, so that we might receive the promised Spirit through faith." The inheritance that Christ possesses belongs to us as well, when we come to be "in Christ." That is true of every Christian believer.

Inspiring Example

Does Christ's own willingness to die inspire his followers to be willing to die for their brothers? It does, according to 1 John 3:16: "By this we know love, that he laid down his life for us, and we ought to lay down our lives for the brothers." We must be careful, however. We cannot imitate Christ in every respect. By his death he atoned for sins. He represented us in a unique way. We cannot atone for sins. And we do not represent anyone else as a sin bearer. But there are *some ways* in which we are supposed to imitate Christ. Christ loved us. We are supposed to love our brothers and sisters in Christ, as 1 John 3:16 indicates. We see a partial pattern of reflections here. As he laid down his life, so we lay down our lives. This pattern is valid. It becomes pernicious only if, as in some forms of modernist theology, it claims to *eliminate* rather than complement the other aspects of Christ's atoning work. Christ is an example to us, in certain aspects of what he has done. In other aspects, he is unique. We cannot become sin bearers in the way that he was. Christ is God and we are not.

An Application

Let us marvel at the unique work that God did for us in giving Christ to us as sin bearer. Let us also marvel at the privilege that is ours to imitate Christ in his love and generosity to us.

15

Already and Not Yet

CLIMACTIC, ETERNAL SALVATION has dawned in Christ. It has dawned, but we still await the consummation when Christ returns. We already can look back on the salvation that Christ has accomplished. We enjoy the "down payment" of his benefits through the presence of the Holy Spirit. Second Corinthians 1:22 says that God has "given his Spirit in our hearts as a *guarantee*" (see also Eph. 1:14). The Greek word for *guarantee* can also mean "down payment," as the ESV indicates in a marginal note.

The idea of "down payment" implies that there are two phases. The first occurs when the down payment is delivered. The second occurs when the rest of the payment is delivered. So there are two phases in working out the redemption that Christ has achieved. There is a phase that is *already* here, because Christ has already died and is already raised from the dead. The Holy Spirit has already been poured out on the day of Pentecost (Acts 2:33). And there is a second phase, which is *yet to come*. This second phase includes the return of Christ, the resurrection of the body, and the establishment of the new heavens and the new earth.

Truth as a Perspective on the Accomplishment of Salvation

We can use truth as a perspective on these events. When Christ came to earth, he accomplished the climactic works of salvation. The accomplishment of salvation, in his work, was accompanied by a fuller manifestation of the truth. Hebrews 1:1–2 indicates the climax:

> Long ago, at many times and in many ways, God spoke to our fathers by the prophets, but in these last days he has spoken to us by his Son, whom he appointed the heir of all things, through whom also he created the world.

Notice how Hebrews 1:1–2 shows the presence of the message of salvation in the prophets, but also emphasizes the supreme manifestation of truth in that "he [God] has spoken to us by his Son." There is progress in revelation. The truth as known by God does not change, but the people of God come to know more. In the New Testament era, truths about God and his salvation are revealed more fully and more deeply than they were in the Old Testament era. The saints in the Old Testament were saved, but their salvation was ultimately based on the work of Christ, who was still to come.

But that is not all. Shadows are superseded by reality. Prefigurations and symbols are displaced by the truths that they anticipated (Col. 2:17). At the heart of it all is the coming of Christ himself. Christ's salvation can be described in many ways. One way is to say that Christ is himself the Truth (John 14:6). He is himself at the heart of the fulfillment of promises made in the Old Testament (2 Cor. 1:20). One aspect of salvation is that God makes himself known to his people in a definitive way:

And no longer shall each one teach his neighbor and each his brother, saying, "Know the LORD," for they shall all know me, from the least of them to the greatest, declares the LORD. (Jer. 31:34)

The fullness of knowing the Lord and his truths belongs to the coming consummation, the new heaven and the new earth (1 Cor. 13:12; Rev. 21:1–2; 22:4–5). But genuine knowledge of his truths also belongs to the present, because those who believe in Christ come to know the Father through him:

All things have been handed over to me by my Father, and no one knows the Son except the Father, and no one knows the Father except the Son and *anyone to whom the Son chooses to reveal him.* (Matt. 11:27)

Jesus said to him, "I am the way, and the truth, and the life. No one comes to the Father except through me. If you had known me, you would have known my Father also. *From now on you do know him* and have seen him." (John 14:6–7)

Jesus as the Focus of Revelation

Jesus is the one who makes the true God known:

No one has ever seen God; the only God, who is at the Father's side, he has made him known. (John 1:18)

And this is eternal life, that they know you, the only true God, and Jesus Christ whom you have sent. (John 17:3)

This knowledge of God that is given to believers comes in two stages. We have entered into knowledge *already*, through the gift of the Holy Spirit. But we will know *yet more fully* when Christ returns. Our present knowledge of the truth is the focus of Hebrews 1:2: "in these last days he has spoken to us by his Son." The future fuller knowledge is in focus in 1 Corinthians 13:12:

> For now we see in a mirror dimly, but then face to face. Now I know in part; then I shall know fully, even as I have been fully known.

In sum, there are two phases in our reception of the truth. In the present phase, we who believe have the truth that God has given us about Christ and his work. But we do not have the truth in perfect fullness. This pattern of two phases is shown not only in two phases of the truth, but also in two phases in other aspects of salvation.

Complementary Aspects of Salvation

It is important to say that salvation does not result only in a narrow intellectual change. Nor does it result merely in having more information. The knowledge of the truth that we gain in salvation is personal knowledge of a personal God. To obtain this knowledge is possible only in fellowship with God. Entering into fellowship can take place only through removal of all the barriers that exist due to God's holiness and our sinfulness. Therefore, events must take place in the world. Jesus must be our sin bearer and must bear our guilt. But these events are themselves part of the truth of salvation, and they are declared in the message of salvation in order that we may know them. God enables us to appropriate the truth intellectually, as well as to experience it in ourselves and to have the riches of personal fellowship with God. So truth can be used as a perspective on the entire scope of salvation.

An Application

God calls us to have joy in the salvation that we have already received:

> These things I have spoken to you, that *my joy* may be in you, and that *your joy* may be full. (John 15:11)

> So also you have sorrow now, but I will see you again, and your hearts will *rejoice*, and no one will take *your joy* from you. (John 16:22)

> Until now you have asked nothing in my name. Ask, and you will receive, that *your joy* may be full. (John 16:24)

> I have said these things to you, that in me you may have peace. In the world you will have tribulation. But take heart; I have overcome the world. (John 16:33)

God also calls us to have patience and hope as we wait for the full application of Christ's salvation, which will come when he returns (Rom. 5:2–4; 8:24–25).

PART IV

APPLICATION OF
REDEMPTION

16

God's Initiative in Saving People

CHRIST HAS ACCOMPLISHED our salvation. But how is it applied? His salvation is comprehensive. Salvation takes care of all the effects of the fall. Christ as the last Adam achieved the dominion that Adam failed to achieve. When we come to Christ, we enter into all the benefits of what he has accomplished. These benefits are many-faceted. Let us consider some of them.

The Coming of the Gospel

As a result of Christ's achievement, the message of the gospel is going out to the world. Christ commissions his disciples to begin in Jerusalem:

> But you will receive power when the Holy Spirit has come upon you, and you will be my witnesses in Jerusalem and in all Judea and Samaria, and to the end of the earth. (Acts 1:8)

The message of the gospel is the message of the truth. It focuses on those central truths that are to be announced, and on calling people to respond to the truth. The truth contains information about what has happened and what God planned and foreknew (Acts 2:23). But this information calls for a response. In that respect, the truth contains the demand for response. And since this truth is spread by the power of the Holy Spirit, the truth has power. The Spirit enables people to respond in faith: "The Lord opened her [Lydia's] heart to pay attention to what was said by Paul" (Acts 16:14).

Effectual Calling

"Effectual calling" is the theological term that has come to be used to describe how God works to bring people to faith. He "calls" them through his voice announcing the gospel. For the call to be "effectual" means that he effectively brings about the intended response. The people who receive an "effectual call" are so stirred up and transformed by the work of God's Spirit that they respond in faith.

But since the fall, human beings in their fallen condition are hostile to the truth. Especially, they are hostile to the truth of the gospel. It seems to them to be folly:

> For since, in the wisdom of God, the world did not know God through wisdom, it pleased God through the folly of what we preach to save those who believe. For Jews demand signs and Greeks seek wisdom, but we preach Christ crucified, a stumbling block to Jews and folly to Gentiles, but to those who are called, both Jews and Greeks, Christ the power of God and the wisdom of God. For the foolishness of God is wiser than men, and the weakness of God is stronger than men. (1 Cor. 1:21–25)

As Ephesians 2:1 puts it, people are "dead in . . . trespasses and sins." This deadness pertains to how they respond to the truth. They are unable to receive it properly—unless, as Ephesians 2:5 points out, they are raised to new life. That resurrection can take place only through Christ: "[he] made us alive together with Christ" (v. 5). New life comes in conjunction with the truth of who God is and what he has done. And in new life new believers embrace the truth. The truth is the truth that comes from the Holy Spirit. And the Holy Spirit has spiritual power to make the truth effective. Effectual calling is a work of the truth, in the power of the Holy Spirit. As the apostle Paul says, "[O]ur gospel came to you not only in word, but also in power and in the Holy Spirit and with full conviction" (1 Thess. 1:5).

Truth That Is Transforming

When truth comes with this power of the Holy Spirit, it is transforming truth. Again, we may underline the fact that this truth does not simply transform people's minds by causing them to have new ideas in their minds. People through faith, by the power of the Holy Spirit, come into spiritual contact with Christ. They have personal union with Christ. They are transformed as *whole people.*

John 3 uses the image of new birth. New birth is a radical picture of newness. Second Corinthians 5:17 uses the language of "new creation." The picture in Ephesians 2:5 is a picture of having been raised to new life together with Christ. Colossians 3:1 presupposes this transition: "If then you have been raised with Christ, seek the things that are above . . ." The transition marked by effectual calling is the beginning of a whole new life, lived on earth, and also anticipating eternal life in the new heaven and new earth.

An Application

Let us thank the Lord that he works in us to cause us to have faith and to come to him. We do not deserve it (Eph. 2:8–9). Let us also pray that God would continue to bring people to faith as the gospel spreads through us, near us, and throughout the world.

17

Justification and Sanctification

WE CONTINUE TO CONSIDER benefits of salvation in connection
with the theme of truth. One benefit is pardon.

Justification

"Justification" is the technical term usually used to summarize the
benefit of full and free forgiveness.[1] For the sake of Christ and his
righteousness, our sins are pardoned, never to be a liability for us
again. Positively, we inherit Christ's righteousness and we have perfect
positive status in the sight of God.

We have already been judged righteous by God's judgment:

Who shall bring any charge against God's elect? It is God who *justi-
fies*. Who is to condemn? Christ Jesus is the one who died—more

---

1 "Justification is an act of God's free grace unto sinners, in which he pardoneth all
their sins, accepteth and accounteth their persons righteous in his sight; not for any
thing wrought in them, or done by them, but only for the perfect obedience and
full satisfaction of Christ, by God imputed to them, and received by faith alone"
(*Westminster Larger Catechism*, A. 70).

than that, who was raised—who is at the right hand of God, who indeed is interceding for us. (Rom. 8:33–34)

In this context, "to justify" is to act as judge in pronouncing a verdict. God says to us who are in Christ, "You are acquitted." Being justified is the opposite of being condemned (Rom. 8:1). The background is found in the pictures offered by human courts of judgment in the Old Testament. The judges are supposed to act with integrity. They are supposed to acquit the innocent and condemn the guilty:

> If there is a dispute between men and they come into court and the judges decide between them, acquitting the innocent and condemning the guilty, . . . (Deut. 25:1; see also Ex. 23:7).

Justification in Relation to the Truth

As we consider these benefits from the perspective of truth, the aspect that stands out is that the pronouncement of the judge is supposed to be in harmony with the truth. The judge is supposed to pronounce the innocent to be innocent ("acquitted") because he is innocent. The judge is supposed to condemn the guilty because he is truly guilty. For a human judge to act otherwise is to pervert justice (Ex. 23:2, 6; Deut. 16:19–20; 24:17).

But now we must ask about the divine judge. God is the archetypal judge. Human judges at their finite level reflect the more ultimate judgment of God. Do different standards apply to God than to human judges? There is a monumental difference, because God is the Creator and is the infinite original. But the justice of God's judgment is precisely the standard by which human judges are supposed to operate. God is a God of truth. So God's judgments will always be in accord with the truth.

That insight affects how we think about pardon for sin. This pardon is not a case where God simply averts his eyes and does not notice the true status of the person he is judging. God does not, in effect, say, "Well, this person is actually guilty of innumerable sins, and deserves death; but I have decided nevertheless to go against my normal standards and let him off."

We can put it in a more striking way. Why did Christ have to die? He had to die because the guilt had to be dealt with:

> upon him was the chastisement that brought us peace,
>   and with his wounds we are healed.
> All we like sheep have gone astray;
>   we have turned—every one—to his own way;
> and the LORD has laid on him
>   the iniquity of us all. (Isa. 53:5–6)

By union with Christ, we *do* have the true status that God the Father pronounces us to have. We are truly innocent, not guilty. It is not because of an inherent goodness that we have by ourselves. It is because of the true righteousness of Christ that is ours. "For our sake he made him to be sin who knew no sin, so that in him we might become the righteousness of God" (2 Cor. 5:21).

As a result, our status of being justified and pardoned is in line with the truth. The justification pronounced by God is a declaration of truth.

Sanctification

"Sanctification" is the usual technical term employed to describe the work of God by which he gradually conforms us more and more to righteousness and holiness.[2] We become more Christlike, in our persons, in our thoughts, and in our behavior. Some people observe that the first step in renewal comes with effectual calling and rebirth. But the word "sanctification" is more often used with respect to the gradual work of God taking place subsequent to the initial work of renewal and conversion.

God's work of renewal and transformation takes place by using the truth. Jesus says, "Sanctify them in the truth; your word is truth" (John 17:17). In the context, he focuses on the words from the Father that he gives to the disciples: "I have given them your word, and the world has hated them because they are not of the world, just as I am not of the world" (v. 14). Earlier, he gives a more extended description of the words of truth that he is giving:

> I have manifested your name to the people whom you gave me out of the world. Yours they were, and you gave them to me, and they have kept your word. Now they know that everything that you have given me is from you. For I have given them the words that you gave me, and they have received them and have come to know in truth that I came from you; and they have believed that you sent me. (vv. 6–8)

In addition, we know that the *standard* for true holiness is found in God's holiness. This holiness is expressed for us in his law, summed up

2 "Sanctification is a work of God's grace, whereby they whom God hath, before the foundation of the world, chosen to be holy, are in time, through the powerful operation of his Spirit applying the death and resurrection of Christ unto them, renewed in their whole man after the image of God; having the seeds of repentance unto life, and all other saving graces, put into their hearts, and those graces so stirred up, increased, and strengthened, as that they more and more die unto sin, and rise unto newness of life" (*Westminster Larger Catechism*, A. 75).

in the Ten Commandments. The truth about God is expressed in the truth of the Ten Commandments. The Ten Commandments supply us with the truth about holiness. Holiness in us is conformity to the truth.

We can arrive at the same conclusion if we notice how Jesus summarizes discipleship. To be his disciple involves loving him and keeping his commandments:

If you love me, you will keep my commandments. (John 14:15)

Whoever has my commandments and keeps them, he it is who loves me. And he who loves me will be loved by my Father, and I will love him and manifest myself to him. (John 14:21)

Whoever does not love me does not keep my words. And the word that you hear is not mine but the Father's who sent me. (John 14:24)

Already you are clean because of the word that I have spoken to you. (John 15:3)

If you abide in me, and *my words* abide in you, ask whatever you wish, and it will be done for you. (John 15:7)

As the Father has loved me, so have I loved you. Abide in my love. If you keep my commandments, you will abide in my love, just as I have kept my Father's commandments and abide in his love. (John 15:9–10)

These verses are *word*-centered statements about discipleship and love. Jesus does not give his words *merely* in order that we would have words and yet not pay attention to them and not keep them. Rather, the words are words of truth, and keeping them is an expression of union with the one who is the Truth (John 14:6). In other words, we must "abide in him," the one who is the true vine (John 15:1–11). We must act truly, even as God, who is the truth himself, acts.

We may put it another way: Sanctification means conformity to Christ, who is our life and our holiness. It is conformity therefore to the truth that is in him (John 14:6; Eph. 4:21).

An Application

Let us seek to grow in Christ by abiding in him and in his word and having it dwell in our heart (John 15:7).

18

The Church

THE CHURCH IS THE BODY OF CHRIST. It is also, according to 1 Timothy 3:15, "a pillar and buttress of the *truth.*" The previous chapters on the application of redemption have focused to some extent on what happens to individual people. But redemption has a corporate dimension as well. When we use truth as a perspective, it reminds us that truth has a corporate dimension.

Sharing in the Truth

The truth is spoken by individual people. But it is also reinforced by conversations and communities. The church is a community crafted by God as "a pillar and buttress of the truth" (1 Tim. 3:15). The truth of the gospel is heard again and again, passed from one member to another. Ephesians 4:11 particularly focuses on people who are especially gifted in handling the truth:

> And he [Christ] gave the apostles, the prophets, the evangelists, the shepherds and teachers.

The very next verses go on to indicate how these people equip others, so that the whole body, working together, enables growth toward maturity:

> to equip the saints for the work of ministry, for building up the body of Christ, until we all attain to the unity of the faith and of the knowledge of the Son of God, to mature manhood, to the measure of the stature of the fullness of Christ. (vv. 12–13)

There is a complex and rich working together. The unity of the body means something in practice.

In Ephesians 4, verses 14–16 further develop a picture in which the truth functions for mutual building up:

> so that we may no longer be children, tossed to and fro by the waves and carried about by every wind of doctrine, by human cunning, by craftiness in deceitful schemes. Rather, speaking the truth in love, we are to grow up in every way into him who is the head, into Christ, from whom the whole body, joined and held together by every joint with which it is equipped, when each part is working properly, makes the body grow so that it builds itself up in love.

We may further confirm the importance of corporate action if we include under the topic of truth the practice of truth in love. "Speaking the truth in love" (v. 15) has a clear role, but then the result includes that the body "builds itself up in love" (v. 16).

The Sacraments

We may also include under the general topic of the church the function of the sacraments, namely baptism and the Lord's Supper. Jesus, by speaking, directed the church to practice these symbolic actions during the time after his death and resurrection (Matt. 28:18–20; Luke 22:19–20; 1 Cor. 11:24–25). So the origin of these symbolic actions lies in truth, the truth that Jesus speaks when he explains the symbolic acts. Jesus's explanation also imparts to the symbolic actions their symbolic value. They mean something. Their meaning lies in what Jesus says about them, plus further explanations given by the New Testament letters, plus background meanings from the Old Testament—cleansing rites in the Old Testament (Heb. 6:2), the "baptism into Moses" at the Red Sea (see 1 Cor. 10:2), the Passover (Luke 22:14–20), and other Old Testament feasts. Thus, the sacraments are bearers of the truth of God, the truth of the gospel.

These aspects of truth show that the sacraments are instruments for conveying truth. One theory, the remembrance theory, says that the whole point of the sacraments is to be a teaching tool, to remind disciples of what Jesus did for them. That is certainly a part of their function. But the signs go together with what they signify. So a recipient who receives the truth in faith, receives Christ and his promises, through the means of the signs. That is, in receiving the truth in faith, he is not only baptized with water, but receives what baptism *signifies*. He is baptized with the Spirit into Christ. He feeds on Christ as he participates in the Lord's Supper. This result is an implication of the active power of the truth, as it comes in the power of the Holy Spirit.

An Application

Let us thank the Lord for giving us the church, brothers and sisters in Christ. Let us determine that we will appreciate the ministry of the truth that comes through the corporate speaking of the truth in the body, as well as in our private reading of the Bible. Let us thank the Lord for giving us the sacraments of baptism and the Lord's Supper.

19

The Consummation

EARLIER, WE SAW that the application of redemption comes in two stages (chapter 15). The climax of redemption is already in the past. Christ has been raised from the dead. But we do not yet see the consummation of redemption.

Consummation and Truth

The consummation is the consummation of the manifestation of truth. The goal of our existence is communion with God. This communion is depicted in Revelation 22:3–4 in terms of the intimacy of face-to-face fellowship:

> No longer will there be anything accursed, but the throne of God and of the Lamb will be in it, and his servants will worship him. They will see his face, and his name will be on their foreheads.

We shall know God more fully: "Now I know in part; then I shall know fully, even as I have been fully known" (1 Cor. 13:12). In the light of the fact that we remain creatures, the verse does not mean that we will have the omniscience of God. But there will be an intense and deep knowledge. This depth of knowledge makes it analogous to the intense and deep knowledge that God has of us. To know truth fully is to know God.

This increase in knowledge is an increase in possession of the truth and enjoyment of the truth. It goes together with a consummate increase in many other aspects of human existence in communion with God.

Judgment

The consummation, as the manifestation of the truth, includes the manifestation of judgment. The last judgment brings to light what has hitherto been hidden:

> And I saw the dead, great and small, standing before the throne, and books were opened. Then another book was opened, which is the book of life. And the dead were judged by *what was written in the books, according to what they had done.* And the sea gave up the dead who were in it, Death and Hades gave up the dead who were in them, and they were judged, each one of them, according to what they had done. (Rev. 20:12–13)

This judgment is a judgment that brings truth to light. It is also a judgment that is in perfect accord with the truth. The judgment is "according to what they had done" (vv. 12, 13). Everyone gets what he or she deserves. All of us would dread the result, were it not for the promise that, in Christ, our names are in the book of life. We are judged according to what we are in Christ, according to the perfection of his righteousness. We are judged according to what is true.

Promise

The manifestation of the truth includes a manifestation of its certainty. It is assured that God will bring about what he has promised:

> And he who was seated on the throne said, "Behold, I am making all things new." Also he said, "Write this down, for these words are trustworthy and true." (Rev. 21:5)

Manifestation of Beauty and Glory

The truth of God is beautiful and glorious. So the manifestation of truth is also a manifestation of beauty and glory. Such, indeed, is the nature of the new world:

> And he carried me away in the Spirit to a great, high mountain, and showed me the holy city Jerusalem coming down out of heaven from God, having the glory of God, its radiance like a most rare jewel, like a jasper, clear as crystal. (Rev. 21:10–11)

> And the city has no need of sun or moon to shine on it, for the glory of God gives it light, and its lamp is the Lamb. (v. 23)

The new world reflects the glory of our most glorious Savior. "The Lord God will be their light" (Rev. 22:5).

An Application

As we read the visions describing the new world, let the words and the truth of the words stir us up to prayer, to good works, and to longing for the coming of the Lord:

> He who testifies to these things says, "Surely I am coming soon." Amen. Come, Lord Jesus! (Rev. 22:20)

Conclusion

WE COULD EXTEND our exploration. Truth is an attribute of God (John 3:33). So it may serve as a perspective on God. And if it is a perspective on God, it may also serve as a perspective on all that God does. It may serve as a perspective on creation and on redemption and on consummation. This use of the theme of truth reminds us of the unity and coherence in God and in his works. His plans encompass all the details of the events of the world (Matt. 10:30). But it is also one plan, in its rational coherence and loving harmony.

God knows exactly what he is doing. That gives us security. He will accomplish exactly what he has planned in his infinite wisdom. That gives us security. His words are true. That gives us security. The whole of it manifests that God is truth (John 3:33). The divine Word is the Truth (John 1:1; 14:6). What he speaks to us is the truth (John 17:17). The whole of history manifests his truthfulness. We can rejoice even now with "joy that is inexpressible and filled with glory" (1 Pet. 1:8).

Bibliography

Augustine. "On the Holy Trinity." In *Nicene and Post-Nicene Fathers*, 1st. series. 3:17–228. Edited by Philip Schaff. London: T & T Clark, 1980.

Boettner, Loraine. *The Reformed Doctrine of Predestination*. Grand Rapids, MI: Eerdmans, 1936.

Frame, John M. *The Doctrine of the Word of God*. Phillipsburg, NJ: P&R, 2010.

Frame, John M. "A Primer on Perspectivalism," 2008, http://frame-poythress.org/a-primer-on-perspectivalism-revised-2008/, accessed Nov. 21, 2016.

Gauger, Ann, Douglas Axe, and Casey Luskin. *Science and Human Origins*. Seattle: Discovery Institute Press, 2012.

Long, V. Philips. *The Reign and Rejection of King Saul: A Case for Literary and Theological Coherence*. Atlanta: Scholars Press, 1989.

Poythress, Vern S. *Chance and the Sovereignty of God: A God-Centered Approach to Probability and Random Events*. Wheaton, IL: Crossway, 2014.

Poythress, Vern S. *God-Centered Biblical Interpretation*. Phillipsburg, NJ: P&R, 1999.

Poythress, Vern S. *Interpreting Eden: A Guide to Faithfully Reading and Understanding Genesis 1–3*. Wheaton, IL: Crossway, 2019.

Poythress, Vern S. *Knowing and the Trinity: How Perspectives in Human Knowledge Imitate the Trinity.* Phillipsburg, NJ: P&R, 2018.

Poythress, Vern S. *Logic: A God-Centered Approach to the Foundation of Western Thought.* Wheaton, IL: Crossway, 2013.

Poythress, Vern S. *The Mystery of the Trinity: A Trinitarian Approach to the Attributes of God.* Phillipsburg, NJ: P&R, 2020.

Poythress, Vern S. "The Quest for Wisdom." In *Resurrection and Eschatology: Theology in Service of the Church: Essays in Honor of Richard B. Gaffin, Jr.,* 86–114. Edited by Lane G. Tipton and Jeffrey C. Waddington. Phillipsburg, NJ: P&R, 2008. https://frame-poythress.org/the-quest-for-wisdom/.

Poythress, Vern S. *Reading the Word of God in the Presence of God: A Handbook for Biblical Interpretation.* Wheaton, IL: Crossway, 2016.

Poythress, Vern S. *Redeeming Mathematics: A God-Centered Approach.* Wheaton, IL: Crossway, 2015.

Poythress, Vern S. *Redeeming Science: A God-Centered Approach.* Wheaton, IL: Crossway, 2006.

Poythress, Vern S. *The Shadow of Christ in the Law of Moses.* Reprint, Phillipsburg, NJ: P&R, 1995 (orig. ed. 1991).

Poythress, Vern S. *Symphonic Theology: The Validity of Multiple Perspectives in Theology.* Grand Rapids, MI: Zondervan, 1987. Reprint, Phillipsburg, NJ: P&R, 2001.

Schaff, Philip. *The Creeds of Christendom: With a History and Critical Notes.* 3 vols. New York: Harper & Brothers, 1890.

Versteeg, J. P. *Adam in the New Testament: Mere Teaching Model or First Historical Man?* Translated by Richard B. Gaffin Jr. Phillipsburg, NJ: P&R, 2012.

Warfield, Benjamin B. *The Inspiration and Authority of the Bible.* Philadelphia: Presbyterian & Reformed, 1948.

Westminster Confession of Faith and Catechisms. https://www.pcaac.org/bco/westminster-confession/, accessed Nov. 4, 2020.

General Index

Adam, 66, 74–77, 80–87, 90–92,
   113–117, 129
   as federal head, 90–92
   historicity of, 77
   and modern science, 76–77
Adam and Eve, 55, 66, 75, 77, 80–81,
   83, 87, 89
Adam in the New Testament (Versteeg),
   77n1
agency (human), 44–47
   as reflection of God's agency, 94, 96
   relationship to truth, 45–46
   in salvation, 101
   as secondary cause, 93
   See also cause/causation; choice; free
      will
Apostles' Creed, The, 19n4
archetype, 76
   See also ectype
atonement, 113–19
   and substitution, 113–14, 116–18
Augustine, 38n3
Axe, Douglas, 77n1

Bethlehem, 21
Bible, authority of, 12, 12n1, 68–69
Boettner, Loraine, 43n1

Cain, 89
cause/causation, 93–98, 100

   and secondary causes, 60, 61, 93
   See also God, and causation; agency
      (human)
Chalcedonian Creed, 107
Chance and the Sovereignty of God
   (Poythress), 43n1, 44n2
choice, 44, 48, 93, 96–97, 99, 101
   See also agency (human)
Christ. *See* Son (Jesus)
church. *See* truth, and church
consummation
   definition of, 143
   and truth, 143–44
covenant, 79–86
   framework of, 86
   in Genesis 2–3, 81–83
   rewards and punishments of,
      83–85
creation/creativity, 53–58
   of mankind, 76, 77
   from nothing, 56
   purpose of, 57
   relationship to science, 57–58
   and revelation, 65–66
   and truth, 53, 66

David, 21, 28, 48–49, 91, 114
death, 80, 83–86, 90, 102, 108, 111, 113,
   116

151

Scripture Index

SCRIPTURE INDEX

Also Available from Vern Poythress

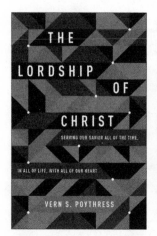

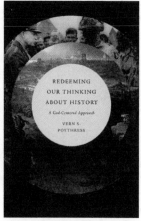

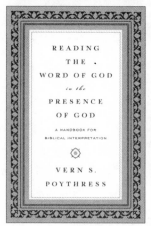

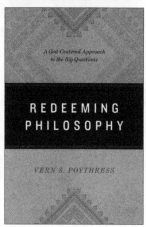

For more information, visit **crossway.org**.